The Tower of London

The Story of
The Tower of London

Tracy Borman

MERRELL
LONDON · NEW YORK

In association with
Historic
Royal Palaces

Contents

Introduction

To know the story of the Tower of London is to be familiar with all the great actors in the drama of English history, for its ancient walls and weather-beaten stones are the links that bind generation to generation and age to age from the Norman Conquest to the present day.

This extract from an early twentieth-century guidebook captures the enormous significance of the Tower of London. It has been not just the backdrop, but also the lead actor in some of the most momentous events of our history. Exploring the stories of its 950-year history reveals a dazzling cast of characters, from the well known (such as Anne Boleyn, Sir Walter Ralegh and the Princes in the Tower) to the more unexpected (spies, jewel thieves and polar bears).

Renowned as a fortress and place of execution, the Tower in fact has a much richer and more complex history. It has been home not only to prisoners and weapons, but also to royal beasts, public records and the nation's coinage. The bewildering array of different operations and institutions to which it has played host has meant that the fortress has been a centre of constant, prolific activity throughout the years.

When building work began on the Tower of London, the capital was little more than a small town, with about 10,000 inhabitants. Some 950 years later, the Tower still stands at the heart of a city of eight million people, as a symbol of royal power, pomp and ceremony, tradition, heritage, military might, treachery and torture. Its myriad roles are reflected in the complex series of buildings that make up this formidable, magnificent fortress – an iconic site that continues to attract millions of visitors from around the world each year.

This book follows a broadly chronological narrative, but includes thematic sections to convey the many and varied stories of the Tower. Together they comprise the remarkable history not just of a fortress, but also of a nation.

1. *A plan of the Tower of London prepared* c. *1597; see fig. 109.*

The Story of The Tower of London

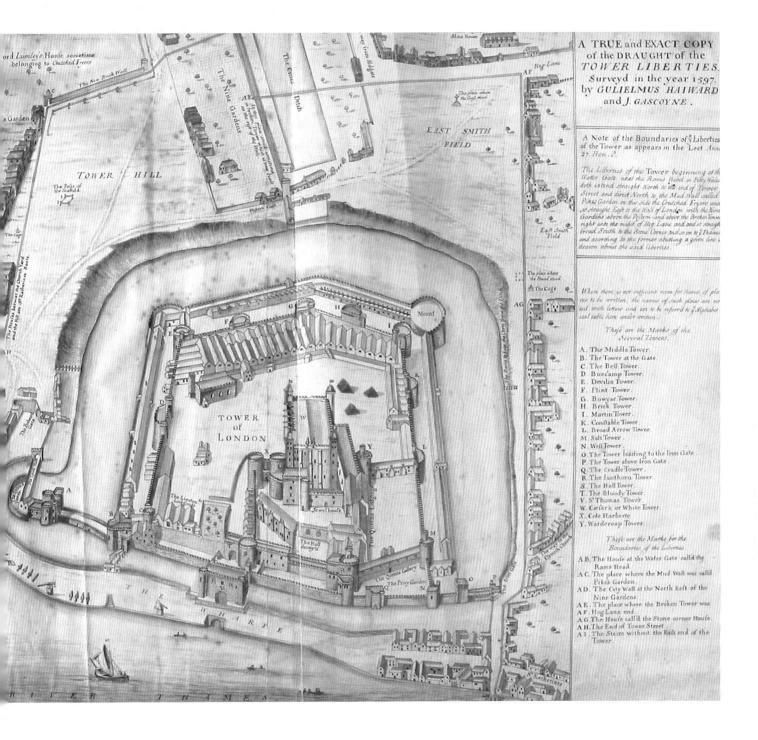

A TRUE and EXACT COPY
of the DRAUGHT of the
TOWER LIBERTIES.
Surveyd in the year 1597.
by GULIELMUS HAIWARD
and J. GASCOYNE.

A Note of the Boundaries of ye Liberties
of the Tower as appears in the Leet Ann.
27. Hen. 8.

The Liberties of the Tower beginning at the
Water Gate next the Rams Head in Petty Wales
doth extend straight North to the end of Tower
Street and direct North to the Mud Wall called
Pikes Garden on this side the Crutched Fryers and
so straight East to the Wall of London with the Nine
Gardens above the Pestern and above the Broken Tower
right unto the midst of Hog Lane and and so straight
broad South to the Stone Corner and so on to ye Thames
and according to the former abutting a green line is
drawn about the said liberties.

Where there is not sufficient room for names of places to be written, the names of such places are noted with letters and are to be referd to ye Alphabet-
ical table here under written:

These are the Marks of the
Several Towers.

A. The Middle Tower.
B. The Tower at the Gate.
C. The Bell Tower.
D. Buscamp Tower.
E. Devilin Tower.
F. Flint Tower.
G. Bowyar Tower.
H. Brick Tower.
I. Martin Tower.
K. Constable Tower.
L. Broad Arrow Tower.
M. Salt Tower.
N. Well Tower.
O. The Tower leading to the Iron Gate.
P. The Tower above Iron Gate.
Q. The Cradle Tower.
R. The Ianthorn Tower.
S. The Hall Tower.
T. The Bloody Tower.
V. St Thomas Tower.
W. Cæsar's, or White Tower.
X. Cole Harbrte
Y. Warderoap Tower.

These are the Marks for the
Boundaries of the Liberties

AB. The House at the Water Gate call'd the
    Rams Head
AC. The place where the Mud Wall was call'd
    Pikes Garden
AD. The City Wall at the North East of the
    Nine Gardens
AE. The place where the Broken Tower was
AF. Hog Lane end.
AG. The House call'd the Stone corner House.
AH. The End of Tower Street.
AI. The Stairs without the East end of the
    Tower.

2. (overleaf) An aerial
view of the Tower from the
south-west; see fig. 50.

The Origins of the Tower

The Tower of London was founded by William the Conqueror after his famous victory at Hastings in 1066, but its story begins many years earlier. The site on which it was built is of Roman origins (fig. 3). The Romans had begun a settlement in London in AD 50, seven years after their invasion of Britain. It occupied a relatively small area (roughly the size of Hyde Park) in what is now the City of London. It is easy to see why they chose this location to establish what would become the foremost city in the kingdom (fig. 4). It was a well-drained and easily defensible site, overlooking marshy ground. The proximity of the River Thames made it easily accessible from the Continent, which aided commerce as well as communication.

But just ten years after its founding, London was destroyed by Boudicca and her forces, who revolted against Roman rule in AD 60. It was quickly rebuilt on a much larger scale, however, and from about AD 70 it became known as Londinium. The Roman historian Tacitus described the city as 'packed with traders'. The wealth that flooded into the city through trade more than justified the expense of the lavish new buildings, which included an amphitheatre, a forum, a basilica (town hall) and public baths. By about AD 80 it also had a bridge across the Thames, close to the site of the present London Bridge.

The earliest known building on the site of the Tower of London dates from the second half of the second century. There are foundations of Roman buildings next to and underneath the White Tower. It was at around the same time that some of the modern street layout was first established, including the route of Great Tower Street, which would later influence the location of the Tower's entrances. The greatest impact on the development of the Tower during this period, however, was the building of a huge defensive wall along the entire landward side of the city. London Wall, as it became known, was more

3. An Iron Age male skeleton, probably dating from just before the Roman invasion, was excavated close to the Lanthorn Tower in 1976. It is one of numerous discoveries that have provided clues to the history of the Tower site.

4. Dating from the late Roman period, this silver ingot was unearthed by workmen digging near the White Tower in 1777. The Romans had a profound impact on the location of the Tower, which incorporated some of the defensive wall that they had built around the capital.

5. (opposite) A section of the City wall at Tower Hill. London Wall, as it became known, was more than 3.2 kilometres (2 miles) long, 6 metres (20 ft) high and 2.4 metres (8 ft) thick. It was completed in around the late second century and would eventually form the Tower's eastern rampart.

The Origins of the Tower

6. *A view of the south-east corner of Roman London and the future site of the Tower of London as it might have looked in about AD 400. The White Tower was later built over the site of the domestic buildings at the top left.*

than 3.2 kilometres (2 miles) long, 6 metres (20 ft) high and 2.4 metres (8 ft) thick (fig. 5). It was completed in around the late second century and would eventually form the Tower's eastern rampart. About a century later, a wall was also built along the riverside. This, too, would later become part of the Tower's defences (fig. 6).

In the late fourth century, the eastern end of the riverside wall, close to the existing Lanthorn Tower, was substantially altered and a massive new wall was built a few metres south of the existing one (fig. 7). This could have been in response to yet another threat of invasion. By this time, the Roman Empire in England was increasingly vulnerable to Germanic invaders (notably the Angles and Saxons), as well as the Picts and Scots. AD 410 is often cited as the date when Roman rule ended in Britain and the country was overrun by

7. The remains of the eastern end of the Roman riverside wall. Originally constructed AD 250–70, it was rebuilt in the late fourth century and formed the Tower's southern rampart until the 1240s. The arcaded wall behind is the inner curtain wall, between the Wakefield and Lanthorn towers.

Germanic tribes. Although London initially went into decline, by AD 600 it had been revived by the East Saxon kings as a major power base. Trading links were rapidly re-established, and the city soon regained its prosperity and vibrancy. Its status was confirmed in 604 by the founding of St Paul's Cathedral. King Alfred took over the city in around 883. Prompted by an attempted Viking invasion the previous year, he set about refortifying it. A palace may also have been built within the old city walls, close to St Paul's.

By 1066 London was the richest and most populous city in the kingdom. The centre of political power had shifted to Westminster, with the creation of the palace and abbey by Edward the Confessor (1042–66). But the area surrounding the Tower remained prosperous enough for an extensive street pattern to have been firmly established, along with two churches: All Hallows and St Peter's (later called St Peter ad Vincula).

The riches of London made it an endlessly attractive prospect for invaders. By the autumn of 1066, the most famous of them all was poised to cross the English Channel.

The Conqueror's Castle

The Tower of London owes its existence to the great conquering king, William, Duke of Normandy (fig. 9). The Normans were renowned for their skill and ruthlessness on the field of combat, and under William's leadership they had become one of the foremost powers of Europe. Their military prowess was complemented by their pioneering use of castles as a means of securing newly won territories – as the citizens of London were about to discover.

In late September 1066 at the port of St Valéry, northern France, Duke William of Normandy was waiting for favourable winds to carry him and his sizeable fleet to England. His Saxon rival, Harold Godwinson, had seized the English Crown on the death of Edward the Confessor in January, and the Duke was one of several foreign powers who resolved to wrest it from him. Even though William, a formidable and greatly feared warrior, had transformed Normandy from a relatively insignificant territory into a power to be reckoned with, his enterprise was still highly risky, and few expected him to succeed.

What followed has become one of the most familiar stories in English history. On 14 October 1066, William defeated King Harold at the Battle of Hastings. The Anglo-Saxon era was at an end: England was

8. (previous pages) The Chapel of St John the Evangelist; see fig. 16.

9. (above) A silver penny from the reign of William the Conqueror (1066–87). The vast majority of William's subjects would have had to rely on such coins to gain an impression of what their new King looked like.

10. William the Conqueror, as depicted in the Bayeux Tapestry. William's claim to the English throne was at best questionable, so the tapestry was part of his propaganda to convince his new subjects of its legitimacy.

now part of the Norman domain. But while the battle had won William the Crown, his campaign to subdue the rest of this hostile, rebellious country was only just beginning (fig. 10). His first priority was to take London, described by a contemporary as 'a most spacious city, full of evil inhabitants, and richer than anywhere else in the kingdom'. The city was so far from accepting the Norman duke as its ruler that it had elected Edgar the Aetheling as king instead. William rapidly assembled his forces and advanced towards it in a circuitous route through Hampshire and Berkshire, intending to cut off support for the city. They brought terror wherever they went, burning entire towns and villages to the ground and murdering their inhabitants. The intimidation tactics worked. When the Normans crossed the Thames at Wallingford, the Archbishop of Canterbury was there to offer his formal submission to Norman rule. Shortly afterwards, a delegation of 'all the chief men from London' met the new King and pledged their allegiance.

11. The Tower as it might have looked in the 1070s or 1080s, with the White Tower under construction. A large outer bailey, which was joined on to the Roman ramparts, covers most of what is now Tower Hill.

The Conqueror's Castle

At the top of the tapestry: ...TEO·DERETVR:CASTELLVM·AT·HESTENGA·CEASTRA   HIC
WII

12. *Another scene from the Bayeux Tapestry, showing the building of a castle at Hastings. Duke William is standing to the centre left. The Normans rapidly built castles across their newly conquered kingdom as a means of securing it.*

13. *William the Conqueror's imposing White Tower, built to subdue the 'evil' inhabitants of London. The original building is very largely intact, with the exception of the turret roofs added by Henry VIII and the surrounds to the windows and doorways.*

Still distrustful of his rebellious new subjects, William sent a contingent of his men ahead 'to build a fortress in the city' and prepare for his arrival. This same tactic was applied in other key towns and cities, and before long the whole kingdom was covered with hastily built but remarkably resilient Norman castles – the finest example of which was soon to appear in London (fig. 12). The Normans' favoured design was 'motte and bailey'. It was ingeniously simple: where there was no natural hill, they made an artificial mound (the motte) and built a wooden tower on top of it. They then dug a defensive ditch around its base (thus forming an enclosure, or bailey), using the excavated earth to make an additional rampart around it. These temporary wooden castles were soon replaced by stone, and fulfilled the dual function of defensive fortress and place of residence for the new Norman magnates.

William's entry into London was quickly followed by his coronation in the newly built Westminster Abbey on Christmas Day 1066. It was a tense, sombre affair, and trouble broke out between William's men and the gathered crowds. The episode strengthened the new King's resolve that the fortresses his men had started building to subdue the 10,000 or so citizens of London should be speedily finished. His chaplain, William of Poitiers, noted that by the time his master left the city soon after his coronation, 'fortifications were being completed as a defence against the numerous and hostile inhabitants'.

The Conqueror's Castle

Two massive strongholds were built at the western and eastern reaches of the city, thus enabling William to hold London in a vice-like grip. The new fortification at the east of the city included an area enclosed by earthworks to the north and west, and by the Roman wall to the south and east. A wooden tower was built in three days in the middle of this rectangular enclosure. Although it was relatively small in size, it was accompanied by a vast but short-lived outer bailey, which contained residential and administrative buildings. This type of fortification was known as 'ringwork', and at least 190 such defences were built by William and his men during the Conquest period.

Although his two new London castles had greatly strengthened Norman rule in London, William was not satisfied. Resolved, perhaps, to create a more visible symbol of Norman domination, he therefore commissioned a huge and imposing new tower to be built in the heart of the new eastern fortification. In around 1075–79 work began on the gigantic keep or 'great tower' (later called the White Tower), which formed the heart of what from the twelfth century became known as the Tower of London (fig. 13).

The building of the White Tower has traditionally been ascribed to Gundulf, Bishop of Rochester. A contemporary chronicler noted that Gundulf supervised 'the king's works on the great tower of London ... for William the Great'. Born in 1024 near Caen in Normandy, Gundulf had entered the Church and became a protégé of Lanfranc, the influential prior of Bec Abbey. He soon demonstrated a talent for architecture. A twelfth-century text describes him as 'competent and skilled at building in stone'. Lanfranc valued him highly, and when he was appointed the first Norman Archbishop of Canterbury in 1070, he brought Gundulf with him to Kent. According to one source, William struck a bargain with Gundulf soon afterwards: he would make him Bishop of Rochester and give him money to restore the cathedral there, so long as he built the new London castle first. Gundulf agreed and was consecrated as Bishop of Rochester in 1077, and work began on the Tower soon afterwards.

The White Tower took more than twenty years to build (although, inexplicably, work was suspended between about 1080 and 1090–93), and it was completed by 1100 (fig. 11). Standing at 27 metres (90 ft) tall, 33 metres (107 ft) wide from east to west and 36 metres (118 ft) wide from north to south, it was one of the largest castle keeps in Europe and dominated the London skyline for miles around. Its massive walls were 4.6 metres (15 ft) thick at their base and 3.4 metres (11 ft) at the top.

Faced with huge blocks of pale marble-like Caen stone imported from Normandy, it presented a dramatic contrast to all of the buildings that surrounded it. The message was clear: the Normans were here to stay.

The key role of the White Tower was defensive. Its scale, the thickness of its walls and the fact that the only entrance was above ground level meant that it was virtually impregnable, and so it would remain throughout its history. The new building was more than just a fortress, however. It probably contained luxury accommodation on the first floor for the royal family and the officer in charge of the castle. The vast rooms within were equipped with fireplaces and latrines (figs. 14 and 15). There was a large hall, which may have been used for ceremonial functions, and a sumptuous chapel, which remains one of the best-preserved Romanesque churches in the country (fig. 16). The entrance floor was reached, as it still is, by an exterior wooden staircase, which could be quickly removed if the castle was under siege. This floor may have originally served as the living quarters of the Tower's garrison, and offered comfortable accommodation. The

14. (above, left) An original latrine in the White Tower – perhaps the earliest known example in the country. Waste was discharged from an opening halfway up the building's outer wall. As the Tower expanded, most of its latrines emptied into the moat.

15. A wall fireplace in the White Tower – another of the sophisticated features of William's new fortress, and one of the earliest examples in England. The smoke would have escaped through small openings in the wall, rather than through a chimney.

16. The Chapel of St John
the Evangelist in the White
Tower. With its eleventh-
century appearance almost
intact, this is one of the
earliest and most beautiful
Romanesque church
interiors in the country.

basement vaults were used for storing food and drink, as well as arms and armour, but later acquired a more sinister reputation as dungeons and torture chambers.

William the Conqueror did not live to see the completion of his 'great tower'. After his death in 1087, he was succeeded by his second surviving son, William Rufus, under whose auspices the White Tower was finished (fig. 17). Although the new King was more preoccupied by improvements to the royal palace of Westminster, he did order reinforcements to the bailey at the Tower. The *Anglo-Saxon Chronicle* for the year 1097 laments the sufferings of the people 'whose labour was due at London' caused by 'the wall ... built about the tower'. They had

son regne, et mist a Caen en normandie

Du roy Guillame

17. William Rufus, who completed the White Tower begun by his conquering father in 1078. A tyrannical and unpopular King, he is shown here burning a town in Normandy, which he attempted to wrest from his brother Robert.

their revenge. Rufus, a tyrant who alienated the Church, nobles and the vast majority of his subjects, was shot while hunting in the New Forest in August 1100. The arrow that pierced his lung was fired by one of the King's own men – probably not by accident.

By commissioning the great hall at Westminster Palace, his principal residence, Rufus had made it clear that the White Tower's primary function was as a fortress. But during the centuries that followed, the distinction between these two roles became increasingly blurred, and the Tower eventually came to fulfil both in almost equal measure – as well as a host of other newly acquired functions. It was a castle of infinite potential, as subsequent monarchs soon came to realize.

The Conqueror's Castle

The Fortress Takes Shape

William the Conqueror had made sure that the Tower was built to last. As a result, his immediate successors carried out little other than minor repairs. His youngest son, Henry I (1100–35), who inherited the throne on the death of Rufus, had a suite of royal lodgings built on the south side of the White Tower.

The turbulence that followed Henry's death in 1135 took the focus away from any further enhancements to the Tower. Henry's two sons, William and Richard, had died when the *White Ship*, which had been carrying them across the Channel from Normandy, sank in 1120 (fig. 18). The country was plunged into civil war when Henry's daughter and heir, Matilda, battled it out with her cousin Stephen, whose claim to the throne rested as much on the general distaste for female rule as on his bloodline.

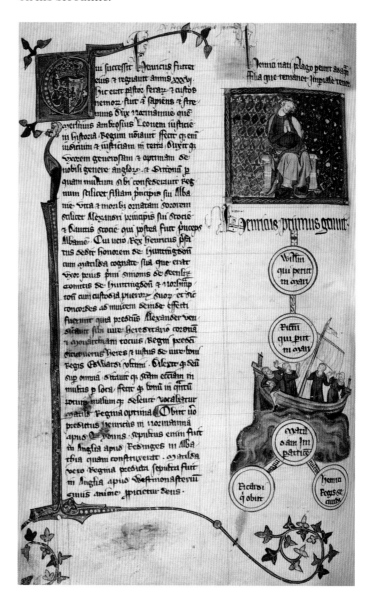

18. In 1120 the sinking of the White Ship, *which carried Henry I's two sons, prompted a succession crisis and plunged the country into civil war. The Keeper of the Tower, Othuer FitzEarl, also died in the wreck.*

The Story of The Tower of London

19. *The Tower's first known prisoner, Bishop Flambard of Durham, escaped in 1101 by climbing through one of the White Tower's windows using a smuggled rope. Illustration from Hutchinson's Story of the British Nation, c. 1920.*

The Fortress Takes Shape

The Tower played a crucial role in the ensuing conflict, which tore England apart for almost two decades. Geoffrey de Mandeville, who was Constable of the Tower for thirteen years, was an unscrupulous baron who helped Stephen to take the fortress – and thus the throne (fig. 20). Stephen (1135–54), meanwhile, became the first monarch to reside in the Tower, and celebrated the Whitsuntide festival there in 1140 in the new royal lodgings built by Henry I.

Although he had been richly rewarded for his service to Stephen, inheriting lands and becoming 1st Earl of Essex, Geoffrey's loyalty was always questionable. When King Stephen gave him the guardianship of Princess Constance, daughter of King Louis VI of France and fiancée of Stephen's eldest son and heir, Eustace, Geoffrey took advantage of the situation. He defied the royal command to release her and instead kept her captive (the first of many royal prisoners at the Tower) until he could be sure who would triumph in the civil war.

When Stephen was defeated and captured by Matilda's forces at Lincoln in 1141, Geoffrey swiftly changed sides and pledged the Tower's allegiance to the new Queen. But he demanded more money and titles in return, as well as permission to strengthen the Tower's defences. These were completed in the nick of time. Matilda's arrogant behaviour had alienated even her own supporters, and Stephen was released shortly afterwards. His followers chased Matilda from the capital and laid siege to the Tower. Geoffrey not only withstood this, but also went on the attack and chased Stephen's forces as far as Fulham, taking the Bishop of London hostage in the process.

Back at the Tower, Geoffrey demanded yet more land from Stephen in return for his dubious loyalty. The King reluctantly agreed, and Geoffrey now became the richest magnate in the kingdom. But Stephen had learned his lesson and would never trust the Constable again. Within a matter of months, Geoffrey was conspiring with Matilda. When Stephen heard of this, he had the Constable arrested in 1143 and stripped of his lands and castles – including the Tower. Unrepentant, Geoffrey whipped up resistance to the Norman regime and remained a thorn in Stephen's side until his death in a skirmish with royal forces in 1144.

20. King Stephen (right) fortified the Tower against the forces of his rival, Matilda. The fortress continued to play an important role during his turbulent reign. Depicted with him is Matilda's son King Henry II, who succeeded Stephen in 1154.

The Story of The Tower of London

Ten years later, Matilda's son was proclaimed Henry II (1154–89), England's first Plantagenet king. Henry's immediate priority was to restore order and stability to his war-torn kingdom. Of key importance was the Tower of London, given that it protected royal authority in the capital. The new King therefore ordered a series of repair works to the fortress. From 1155 these works were supervised by Henry's chief minister and favourite, Thomas Becket, Archbishop of Canterbury, who became Constable of the Tower in 1161 (fig. 21). Becket's contemporary biographer, William Fitzstephen, described the fortress after the completion of the works as 'great and strong with encircling walls rising from a deep foundation and built with mortar tempered with the blood of beasts'. He was referring to the Roman bricks and tiles, which had been ground into a reddish powder to make the mortar, thus giving the White Tower its dramatically contrasting red and white façades.

Henry II's eldest son and heir, Richard 'the Lionheart' (1189–99), spent only a few months in England during his entire reign. Conscious that his younger brother John had his eyes on the throne, Richard commissioned a programme of major building work at the Tower, which was still seen as the key to London – and thus to England. This was superintended by his chief minister, William Longchamp, who was also the Constable of the Tower and effective ruler of the kingdom.

It was under Longchamp's supervision that the Tower began to take the shape that we know today (fig. 22). He almost doubled the size of the fortress by extending the south curtain wall westwards along the river and reinforcing it with a new polygonal tower, the Bell Tower, at its south-west corner (figs. 23 and 24). He probably also commissioned the Wardrobe Tower, which lay on the east of the White Tower. The twelfth-century chronicler Roger of Howden recorded that Longchamp also 'caused the Tower of London to be surrounded by a moat of great depth'. Impressive though it was, it apparently failed to flood, which rather undermined its usefulness.

Longchamp's improvements had antagonized the local population because they involved the destruction of nearby houses. The chronicler William of Newburgh claimed that Longchamp had become 'an intolerable tyrant' by this time. In 1191 Richard's brother John

21. *Thomas Becket was Constable of the Tower in 1161 until he became Archbishop of Canterbury the following year. This fifteenth-century manuscript shows his assassination by four of Henry II's knights, who believed the King had sanctioned it.*

22. *A reconstructed view of the Tower from the south-west, c. 1200. New defences have been added, including the Bell Tower, shown at the bottom left. The Great Hall and other residential buildings are immediately to the south of the White Tower.*

capitalized on the minister's unpopularity and launched an attack on the Tower. The new defences held firm, but Longchamp did not. He surrendered the Tower and went to Dover, from where he attempted to escape to the Continent disguised as a woman, but suffered the humiliation of being propositioned by a fisherman. Although Richard returned to England in 1194 and seized control from John, he never regained his subjects' trust. He died without heirs in 1199, leaving the throne to his rebellious brother.

John (1199–1216) had evidently become fond of the Tower by that time, because he stayed there more than almost any other monarch, either before or since. He may have established the famous Tower Menagerie: certainly he paid for an 'allowance for the keepers of the lion and for the lion itself' (see pages 30–37). But there is no evidence that he made any architectural improvements or additions to the fortress. The only recorded building project was the construction of a 'mud

wall ... between the Tower and the City' in 1214–15, although its purpose is unknown.

As King, John soon became dangerously unpopular. In 1215 his barons rebelled and forced him to issue the Magna Carta. For the first time in English history, legal limits were placed on royal power and new strictures put in place to ensure justice for all the King's subjects. But it soon became clear

that John had no intention of keeping his end of the bargain, and the country was plunged into civil war again. Legend has it that the leader of the rebel barons, Robert Fitzwalter, had particular reason to resent the tyrannical King. In 1214 John had taken a fancy to Robert's eldest daughter, 'Maud the Fair', but the baron had refused to let him take her as his mistress. Furious, John seized the girl and had her imprisoned alone in the highest point of the White Tower. Meanwhile, he sent troops to sack her father's fortress, Baynard's Castle, further west in the city, and Fitzwalter was forced to flee to France. Maud resisted all of the lecherous King's attempts to seduce her. John stepped up the pressure by attempting to starve her into submission. When she continued to hold firm, he was said to have ordered his servants to give her a poisoned egg. The famished girl ate it and suffered a painful death.

Fitzwalter had his revenge. A year later, he and his fellow barons seized control of the Tower and invited Prince Louis, heir to the kingdom of France, to take the throne. The fortress remained their headquarters until May 1217, when the supporters of John's son and heir, Henry III (who had been proclaimed King on his father's death the previous year), triumphed over Louis at the Battle of Lincoln. This dramatic episode made a powerful impression on the young King, who realized just how crucial the Tower was to royal authority.

23. The lower room of the Bell Tower, built during the reign of King Richard in the late twelfth century. Its most famous prisoner was Sir Thomas More, who was kept here from 1534 until his execution the following year.

24. The Bell Tower. Built by William Longchamp in the late twelfth century, this large polygonal Tower was originally on the river's edge at the south-west corner of the fortress. Primarily defensive, it also contained accommodation.

In Focus
The Menagerie

By the time that the Tower Menagerie was established in the early thirteenth century, the keeping of animals by members of the royal family was no great novelty. Henry I had had a private collection of exotic beasts at Woodstock Palace in Oxfordshire, including 'lions, leopards, lynxes, camels, animals which England does not produce'. He also had 'a creature called a porcupine ... an animal covered with bristly hairs which it naturally darts against the dog when pursuing it'.

It was not until the reign of King John that the havoc caused by such 'strange beasts' became the problem of the Tower of London. Upon finally losing Normandy in 1204, John brought back a bizarre consolation prize: three crate-loads of wild beasts. These were probably housed at the Tower. Accounts from 1210 include payments to the Constable, John FitzHugh, relating to the wages of the lion-keepers (fig. 25).

John's son, Henry III, embraced this aspect of the Tower's role with enthusiasm, and it was during his reign that the royal Menagerie was fully established. The inspiration was a gift from overseas. In 1235 Henry's sister Isabella married the Holy Roman Emperor, Frederick II, known throughout Europe as *stupor mundi* ('the wonder of the world'). The wedding at Worms Cathedral was a lavish affair. As well as arranging a gargantuan feast, Frederick also brought with him a selection of animals from his private menageries for his guests' entertainment. They included three wildcats, which he generously decided to give to his new brother-in-law. This was likely to have been a reference to the Plantagenet arms, which included three lions.

Henry was delighted with the gift and arranged for the animals to be brought to the Tower, where a makeshift home was constructed for them. William de Botton, a member of the royal household, was given the dubious honour of looking after the beasts. They survived until at least 1240 and then disappeared from the records. But by then the Tower Menagerie had become more firmly established. The wildcats (or leopards, as they were also called) were soon joined by a lion, and in 1252 Henry ordered that the royal beasts that still lived at Woodstock should be brought to the Tower. This must have presented a challenge to the unfortunate servants who had to ensure the safe carriage of the lynxes, leopards, lions and camels over the 97-kilometre (60-mile) journey.

That same year, Henry received a gift from the King of Norway of a 'pale bear', probably a polar bear. It instantly captivated the citizens of London, who had never seen anything like it before. The Sheriffs of the

City of London were asked to provide money towards the animal's food and keep. This evidently proved a costly business, because after a year or so the people of London were instructed to buy a muzzle, chain and rope so that the bear could fish for its own food in the Thames. The river was a good deal cleaner than it is today and filled with a variety of fish, including 'fat and sweet salmons'. The polar bear must have been delighted. Its keeper was a good deal less so, for there is evidence to suggest that he was expected to accompany his charge on its fishing expeditions.

25. One of two north African Barbary lion skulls excavated from the Tower moat in 1937 and now in the collection of the Natural History Museum. Carbon dating has revealed that one of the lions lived between 1420 and 1480; the other lived between 1280 and 1385, making it the oldest lion found in the United Kingdom.

An even stranger sight confronted the people of London in 1255, when a new and altogether larger gift arrived from the French King, Louis IX. The chronicler Matthew Paris could barely find the words to describe it: 'The beast is about ten years old, possessing a rough hide rather than fur, has small eyes at the top of its head, and eats and drinks with a trunk.' England had welcomed its first elephant (fig. 26).

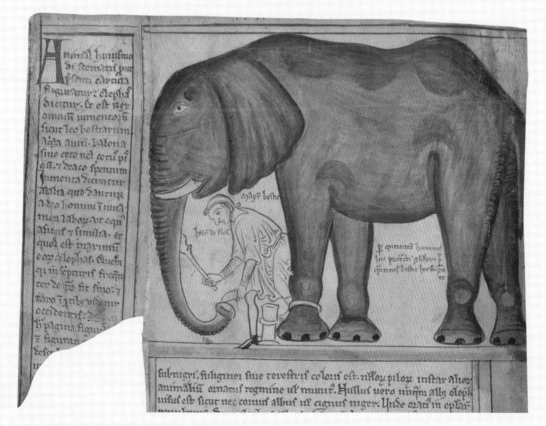

26. An illustration by the chronicler Matthew Paris showing the elephant presented to Henry III by the King of France in 1255. The elephant's keeper, Henry of Flores, is also depicted in order to demonstrate the size of the animal. It died just two years after arriving at the Tower.

27. (opposite) A poster advertising the Tower Menagerie in 1826, by which time it had been greatly expanded by Chief Keeper Alfred Cops. Under his stewardship, the Menagerie experienced prolific growth, and a staggering 300 specimens from sixty different species were housed there.

28. *The lions' den in 1779, showing the two-storey cages that had occupied the Lion Tower since at least the sixteenth century. Lions were some of the first animals to arrive at the Tower Menagerie, and they held an enduring appeal for visitors.*

Sadly, despite the best intentions of the King, who appointed a spacious house for the beast and ensured that it had every possible comfort, the elephant died just two years after arriving at the Tower. Its gigantic carcass was buried close to the Chapel of St Peter ad Vincula, which would later house the headless bodies of Anne Boleyn, Catherine Howard and other victims of Henry VIII's brutal regime. Just a year later, however, the elephant's bones were dug up and sent to Westminster Abbey (which Henry III was in the process of rebuilding), and carved into reliquaries and caskets to house saints' relics.

Perhaps inevitably, given the lack of knowledge about the animals' diet and their care, the lives of the Tower beasts were often short. But the Menagerie continued to thrive, and the changing title of its superintendent – from 'Keeper of His Majesty's Lions and Leopards' to 'Master of the King's Bears and Apes' – reflects the increasing diversity of the occupants.

Edward I created a permanent new home for the Menagerie at the western entrance to the Tower, in what became known as the Lion Tower (fig. 28). It was used to house the animals from the reign of his son, Edward II. The gateway was now the only way into the Tower complex, so any visitors had to pass by the terrifying sight and sound of the wild animals. This was no doubt intended as much to intimidate as to impress them.

The Lion Tower would remain home to the Menagerie for almost six centuries. Although its occupants had been a feared and respected curiosity at first, they gradually became the subject of barbarous entertainment. One of the favourite sports was to bait the lions with vicious mastiff dogs. When Henry VII witnessed this, he was 'deeply displeased' and immediately ordered the hounds to be put to death. Few other monarchs had such scruples. The sadistic James I became a regular visitor to the Tower Menagerie and delighted in watching the animals tearing one another to pieces. He even had a new viewing platform built so this gruesome sport could be more closely observed.

James's bloodlust was not always sated. In 1605 he ordered a live lamb to be lowered into the lions' den on a rope. But instead of devouring the poor creature, the lion 'very gently looked upon him and smelled upon him without sign of any further hurt'. Eventually, the disappointed King conceded that the lamb could be winched back to safety, 'in as good a plight as he was set down'.

Tragedy befell the Menagerie in 1609, when a bear killed a child who had been negligently left in its yard. The King ordered that the bear be punished by being made to fight a lion. But again he was disappointed when the lion proved disinclined to engage in combat. Not to be denied, James ordered that the bear be baited to death by mastiffs instead. The bloody spectacle was watched by the entire royal family, and the benevolent King gave the child's grieving mother a cut of the profits from the ticket sales.

Despite the ill-treatment that the lions in particular received, a tradition had sprung up of naming them after the sovereign. It was believed that if a lion died, then its namesake would soon follow. This superstition endured until at least the eighteenth century. In 1758 the courtier and gossip Lord Chesterfield reported that many of 'the common people' feared that George II was on the point of death because 'one of the oldest lions in the Tower – much about the king's age – died a fortnight ago!' In fact, the King lived for a further two years.

Meanwhile, the diversity of the creatures housed in the Tower Menagerie continued to grow. In 1597 a Czech visitor to London recorded seeing, among other animals, 'a huge porcupine'. This was an exceptionally rare beast in Elizabethan England, so it is possible that Shakespeare had seen the same one in the Tower, because he mentions a porcupine in his most famous play, *Hamlet*. By 1622 the collection had been extended to include three eagles, two pumas, a tiger and a jackal, as well as the obligatory leopards and lions.

29. *Illustrations from* Curiosities in the Tower of London, *a children's guidebook published in 1741, showing animals in the Menagerie. The animals were extremely popular with younger visitors, some of whom fell foul of the more dangerous inhabitants.*

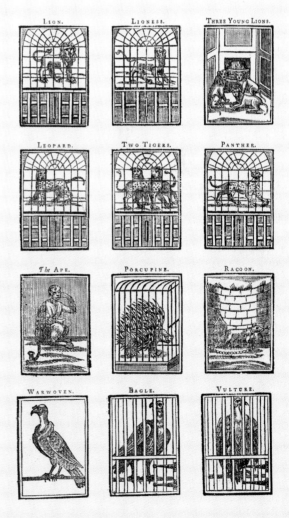

30. (below) The School of Monkeys, a cartoon by Thomas Rowlandson, showing visitors mingling freely with apes in the Menagerie's 'monkey room' in the late eighteenth century. This practice was brought to an abrupt end after a boy was mauled by an ape.

31. An excerpt from a late eighteenth-century children's booklet reporting the escape from the Tower Menagerie of a leopard, which had apparently been deposited there for safe keeping. The leopard is depicted on the wall of the eighteenth-century guardhouse.

TRIFLES
FOR CHILDREN.

PART III.

News from the Tower!

SINCE we publiſhed the Second Part of Trifles for Children, one night a large leopard eſcaped from its den in the Tower of London, where it had been left by a gentleman. At firſt it attacked a

A

Later that century, the famous London diarist Samuel Pepys recorded many visits to the Tower Menagerie. He was particularly fond of an old lion called Crowly, 'who has now grown a very great lion and very tame'. Not all of the beasts were so docile. In 1686 Mary Jenkinson, the servant of the Menagerie Keeper, William Gill, went to stroke one of

The Story of The Tower of London

the lions' paws: 'Suddenly he catched her by the middle of the arm with his claws and mouth, and most miserably tore her Flesh from the Bone, before he could be unloosed, notwithstanding that they thrust several lighted torches at him.' Surgeons were hastily summoned and what was left of Mary's arm was amputated, but the girl died shortly afterwards.

The residents of the Tower Menagerie could be malodorous as well as dangerous. In 1704, in the reign of Queen Anne, one visitor recorded that as well as two Swedish owls and two 'very cruel' mountain cats, there was a jackal whose 'rank smell ... hath much injured the Health of the man that attends them, and so stuffed up his Head that it affects his speech'.

Thanks to the Menagerie, by this time the Tower had begun to emerge as the country's leading tourist attraction – a status that it enjoys to this day, albeit for very different reasons. Zoos became very fashionable during the eighteenth century, and the Tower Menagerie remained pre-eminent. An illustrated children's guide to the zoo was published in 1741, and included pictures of all the animals that could be seen there (fig. 29). Among the most popular were Marco and Phillis, a lion and lioness; a panther called Jenny; a leopard called Will; and a bird of prey called Warwoven. A cartoon by the celebrated caricaturist Thomas Rowlandson shows visitors mingling with apes in the Menagerie's 'monkey room', which opened in the 1780s (fig. 30). But this daring experiment was brought to an abrupt end when a boy was mauled by an over-enthusiastic ape, and the animals were put back in their cages soon afterwards.

Towards the end of the eighteenth century the celebrated poet and painter William Blake paid a visit to the Menagerie. The tiger so captured his imagination that he made an engraving of it to accompany his famous poem in *Songs of Experience* (1794; fig. 32). Scientists also made use of the Menagerie. John Hunter, a respected Scottish surgeon and anatomist, struck a deal with the Keeper John Ellys, who provided the carcasses of dead animals for dissection during the 1750s. The celebrated animal artist Sir Edwin Landseer frequently visited the Menagerie during the 1820s, and the lions there inspired his famous sculptures at the foot of Nelson's Column in Trafalgar Square (fig. 33).

By the beginning of the nineteenth century, however, the Tower Menagerie was in decline. The collection had shrunk to just a handful of animals by 1822 and looked set to die out altogether. But it was saved by the able and energetic zoologist Alfred Cops, who was appointed Chief Keeper that year. Cops immediately set about a programme of

32. 'The Tyger' by William Blake, who was inspired to write this famous poem when he visited the Tower Menagerie towards the end of the eighteenth century. Despite being hailed as 'far and away the greatest artist Britain has ever produced', Blake was largely unrecognized in his own lifetime.

33. *The celebrated animal artist Sir Edwin Landseer was a frequent visitor to the Tower Menagerie during the 1820s, and drew inspiration for his famous lion sculptures in London's Trafalgar Square.*

34. *A contemporary illustration of an 'Extraordinary and fatal combat' between a lion, a tiger and a tigress in December 1830. The caption relates that the 'Lion was so seriously injured that he died in a few days afterwards.'*

The Story of The Tower of London

acquisitions, even travelling the world himself to look for new species. Within six years of his appointment a staggering 300 specimens from sixty different species were housed in the Menagerie, including kangaroos from Australia (fig. 27). The new residents enjoyed a much healthier lifestyle, thanks to Cops's superior knowledge of their diet and welfare. Because of their number, however, they lived in rather cramped conditions – with often fatal results (fig. 34). An inquisitive secretary bird had its head bitten off when it peered into the den of a hyena.

MISERIES OF SOCIAL LIFE.

The wide variety of new animals at the Tower Menagerie made it a thriving tourist attraction once more (fig. 35). But it also sparked unease among the growing number of people who campaigned for animal welfare. The RSPCA had been founded in 1824, and an Animal Protection Act was passed, giving rights to farm and domestic animals. Two years later, the Duke of Wellington – hero of Waterloo – was appointed Constable of the Tower. Motivated less by animal welfare than by his determination to restore the fortress to its military role, he arranged the transfer of 150 of the Menagerie's inhabitants to the Zoological Gardens in Regent's Park, which opened in 1828.

Cops reduced the entry fee to compensate visitors, but he was fighting a losing battle. Several incidents – including an escapee wolf that almost devoured a child, and a monkey that bit a guardsman's leg – convinced King William IV to close the Menagerie for good in 1835. The remaining animals were sold to zoological societies and private collectors, and the Lion Tower was later demolished. In 2011 some of the Tower's former animals came back in sculpture form (fig. 181), peering over the battlements and staring menacingly at visitors, as they did in their heyday.

35. An engraving of 1807 by Thomas Rowlandson, showing visitors arriving from Tower Hill at the Menagerie gate. On the right is a sign directing visitors to the 'Wild Beasts'. Through the archway can be seen the Middle Tower (left) and the Menagerie Keeper's house (right).

In Focus: The Menagerie

Fortress and Palace

Henry III (1216–72) is not renowned for many things; indeed, most people would struggle to name anything of note that happened during his long reign. But he did have one claim to fame: it was he who, after William the Conqueror, did most to shape the Tower of London as we know it today (fig. 38).

36. (previous pages)
A reconstruction of the Tower in the mid-thirteenth century; see fig. 45.

37. (below) Thirteenth-century stonemasons at work. It was during this period that the Tower took the shape that we still recognize today. Architecture was the great passion of Henry III, and he employed a host of masons, carpenters and other craftsmen to transform his London fortress.

38. Henry III (shown here at his coronation) did more to shape the Tower as we know it today than any other monarch except William the Conqueror. His improvements included the addition of ten towers and a new moat, which was flooded successfully for the first time.

The new King's inheritance was hardly enviable. Loyalty to the Crown was at an all-time low, and most of the country was in the hands of the barons who had rebelled against his father, King John. Worse still, Henry was just nine years old when he was proclaimed King, and the accession of a minor typically sparked instability as those about him battled for supremacy. But Henry was fortunate in his chief advisers, Hubert de Burgh and the great soldier William Marshal. They quickly re-established royal authority and – crucially – regained control of the Tower of London (fig. 39).

Having spent most of his young life surrounded by powerful men, Henry himself grew up to be a weak and rather petulant ruler, more interested in religious and aesthetic pursuits than in governing his country. His passion for art and architecture found full expression in the massive programme of building that he began at the Tower during the 1220s (fig. 37). As well as strengthening the castle against invasion or rebellion, Henry made it into a more sumptuous royal residence.

39. The earliest known illustration of the Tower of London, from a late fifteenth-century book of poems by Charles, Duke of Orléans. London Bridge and the city are shown in the background. In 1261 Londoners complained that the Constable of the Tower was impounding merchant ships on the Thames and selling their cargoes. Because of its location, the fortress played a crucial role in commerce, as well as defence, throughout much of its long history.

40. (below) The west side of the Wakefield Tower, built by Henry III in the thirteenth century as part of an ambitious programme of improvements to the fortress. The gateway to his former watergate, the Bloody Tower, is on the left.

41. One of the first-floor rooms in the Salt Tower, built c. 1240. Although primarily defensive, the tower was equipped with such creature comforts as a fireplace, a built-in latrine and a large window overlooking the river.

Three new towers – the Salt, Lanthorn and Wakefield – were rapidly completed and formed part of the southern, riverside curtain wall, which was extended eastwards by 50 metres (164 ft; fig. 41). The largest of these was the octagonal Wakefield Tower, which contained a luxurious bedroom for Henry III, complete with fireplace, oratory and large windows (figs. 40 and 88).

To the north and east of the White Tower, meanwhile, a new curtain wall was built. It was crowned by a range of new towers: (from west to east) the Devereux, Flint, Bowyer, Brick, Martin, Constable and Broad Arrow. These towers were typical of Henry's approach to the fortress, for they fulfilled both a defensive and a residential function, being equipped with arrow slits on their sides and lodgings in their upper chambers.

At the same time, an expert Flemish ditch-digger, who is cited in the records as 'Master John', was employed to improve the moat outside the inner curtain wall (which was then the outer wall), and this time it was successfully flooded. This ambitious programme of building work transformed the Tower into a vast, impregnable fortress, surrounded by a moat on three sides and by the River Thames on the fourth (fig. 42).

Henry III made more aesthetic alterations, too. These included an order 'to have the Great Tower whitened both inside and out' so that it could be seen for miles around, bright and glimmering – thus inspiring the name by which it would later become known. He also commissioned a suite of luxurious private quarters for himself and his new wife, Eleanor of Provence, whom he married in 1236 when he was twenty-eight and his bride only about twelve years old. He decorated the private chamber of his beautiful young wife with a mural of roses on a white background. The King celebrated their wedding by ordering a second coronation. He and his Queen set out from the Tower to Westminster for the ceremony, thus establishing the tradition that all monarchs would spend the night before their coronation in the fortress.

True to his pious reputation, the other addition that Henry made to the Tower was to renovate the Chapel of St Peter ad Vincula (St Peter in Chains). Originally a parish church lying outside the fortress, it had been brought within the complex by the gradual extension of the Tower's defences during the twelfth century. The King now issued detailed instructions for its redecoration. The figures of saints were to be 'newly coloured, all with the best colours ... also

42. An artist's impression of Henry III's new riverside defences. The Bell Tower is on the left, and in the middle is the watergate that was later incorporated into the Bloody Tower. Next to that is the Wakefield Tower, and on its right is the building that would later house the government's records.

two fair cherubim with cheerful and pleasant countenances to be placed on either side of a great crucifix'. Henry also presented his new chapel with a peal of bells. Meanwhile, the White Tower chapel was adorned with new stained-glass windows and decorated with paintings and statues.

Not all of Henry's alterations were successful. The chronicler Matthew Paris recorded that in the year 1240, 'on the evening of the Feast of St George [23 April], the stonework of a certain noble gateway which the king had constructed in the most opulent fashion collapsed, as if struck by an earthquake, together with its forebuildings and outworks'. Henry wasted no time in having the gateway rebuilt, 'more soundly this time and at still greater cost'. But a London priest claimed that Thomas Becket had told him in a dream that the disaster would recur exactly a year later. Sure enough, a year to the day since the first mishap, 'the walls which had been built around the Tower collapsed irreparably' (figs. 44 and 45).

Quite where this ill-fated gateway had been situated remained a mystery until 1995–97, when archaeological investigations revealed a massive stone platform in the moat, just west of the existing outer curtain wall and about 30 metres (98 ft) north-west of the Beauchamp Tower. The thirteenth-century style of its masonry, the fact that it

43. An illustration from Matthew Paris's Greater Chronicle, *showing a Welsh prince, Gruffydd ap Llewelyn, falling to his death while attempting to escape from the Tower in 1244. He tied together sheets, but they unravelled during his descent.*

44. Another illustration from Paris's Greater Chronicle, *showing the collapse of Henry III's western defences at the Tower in 1241. They had first collapsed exactly one year before, but the King had had them swiftly rebuilt. This latest catastrophe proved a major setback to Henry's refortification programme.*

sloped at an alarming angle, and the dating of the timbers driven into the ground behind it, left little doubt that this was part of Henry's collapsed defences.

This major setback dramatically slowed the progress of the King's refortification. Even as late as 1253, when he ordered the Constable to fortify 'the whole breach of the bailey with a wooden stockade', the masonry defences were still incomplete. But by then, the Tower had assumed a new function that had an immediate impact on its increasingly complex suite of buildings.

In the twelfth and early thirteenth centuries, the royal finances had been managed by the Chamber – so called because the king's money had been stored in his private room. His household goods, weapons and valuables, meanwhile, were supervised by the Wardrobe, which by the 1220s or 1230s had been established as an independent organization. It was divided into two parts – one responsible for such perishable goods

45. A reconstruction of the Tower just before the collapse of 1241. The fortress has been greatly enlarged by Henry III, and a new moat is being dug. A new wall is under construction to the north. The twin-towered gateway and the Barbican tower shown on the lower left were on the verge of collapse.

as food, and the other for other valuables, including jewels, clothing, furniture, weaponry, wax and spices. By the 1240s the Tower had become the principal storehouse for this latter category, and Henry III was issued with a key to it in 1249. Four years later, the stores and the body of staff that managed them were being referred to as the Great Wardrobe. From that time, the Great Wardrobe, the Privy Wardrobe (a subsidiary), and the latter's descendants, the Armoury and Board of Ordnance, would have a profound impact on the Tower's role and architecture until as late as the nineteenth century.

King Henry would spend the rest of his reign making improvements to the Tower (fig. 46). By the time of his death, he had spent the considerable sum of £9000 (around £4.8 million today) on shaping the Tower into the magnificent residence and fortress that is recognized by modern-day visitors.

But if Henry had left an impressive legacy in bricks and mortar, his reign had degenerated into the same civil conflict that had ruined his father. By 1261 he had become a virtual prisoner in the Tower – the only place where he could feel safe – and he hastily ordered new fortifications to withstand the attacks of his rebellious barons. In 1263 the King and Queen were holed up in the fortress while their son and heir, Prince Edward, fought the barons in the West Country. Simon de Montfort, leader of the rebels, proposed a humiliating peace, to which Henry was willing to accede. Not so his wife. Resolved to join her son Edward at Windsor, Eleanor set sail from the Tower up the Thames but made it

vant il ont fait le fai-

only as far as London Bridge, where she was beaten back by an angry mob of baronial supporters, who hurled sticks, stones, rotten eggs and other detritus at her barge. She hastily retreated to the Tower, but her ungallant and cowardly husband refused to open the gates to her, fearing that the rebels would burst in behind her. The Lord Mayor of London finally offered her sanctuary at St Paul's.

Three days later, the King submitted to the truce, but trouble soon flared up again, and for the remainder of his reign a vicious and bloody conflict raged between Henry and his barons (fig. 47). It was only thanks to the impenetrable walls of his beloved Tower, together with the valiant efforts of his warlike son Edward, that Henry was able to cling on to power and die a peaceful death in 1272.

47. One of the Tower's most violent sieges took place in 1267, when the fortress was successfully defended by the capital's Jews and the Papal legate. But just eleven years later, Edward I persecuted much of London's Jewish community and had 600 of them imprisoned in the Tower.

Rebels and
Favourites

Edward I (1272–1307) – nicknamed 'Longshanks' because of his tall, imposing frame – was as different from his father as it was possible to be (fig. 49). Ruthless, determined and able, he was of the same mould of warrior-king as William the Conqueror. During the first twenty years of his reign he built a series of great castles – Flint, Caernarfon and Beaumaris being among the most impressive – in order to bring the Welsh to heel. In this, at least, he shared something in common with his father. But while Henry's architectural creations had been designed with comfort and splendour in mind, his son's fulfilled a purely military purpose. Little surprise, then, that when he turned his attention to the Tower of London, his aim was to make the already mighty fortress utterly impregnable (fig. 50).

48. (previous pages) The royal bedchamber inside St Thomas's Tower, re-presented as it would have been in the time of Edward I. Although the King commissioned this luxurious suite of rooms, he rarely made use of it.

49. (right) Edward I and his beloved Queen, Eleanor of Castile, from a fourteenth-century chronicle of his life. This ruthless warrior-king, nicknamed 'Longshanks' because of his imposing frame, strengthened the Tower's defences and extended the royal apartments.

50. An aerial view of the Tower of London from the south-west in 2004. The Tower stands as a bastion of history in the heart of the capital's modern financial district. Its basic layout has remained unaltered since the reign of Edward I.

51. *The small chapel, or oratory, in the north-east turret of St Thomas's Tower, which was built for the King's private use. It led off one of his private rooms, making it easily accessible.*

52. Exit chutes for a series of latrines in Brass Mount, a large bastion built by Edward I at the north-east corner of his new outer curtain wall. The waste would have emptied into the King's new moat, as it did from other latrines in the fortress until the 1840s, when the resulting pollution contributed to the decision to fill in the moat.

Having repaired the damage caused by the last siege on the Tower during his father's reign, Edward employed the expert moat-builder Master Walter to build a large moat outside the present outer curtain wall. As well as defending the fortress, the impressive new moat (which measured 49 metres/160 ft across) also helped to feed those within: the King stocked it with a large number of pike brought from Cambridge. Meanwhile, he encircled the entire Tower complex with a second curtain wall, thus creating a 'concentric' castle, in which one wall encircles another (fig. 52). The same design had

53. St Thomas's Tower, built by Edward I in the 1270s to provide a gateway to the river, as well as comfortable royal accommodation. It was through this gateway that most prisoners would arrive for their incarceration (or worse), and it is for this reason that it later became known as Traitors' Gate.

characterized his great Welsh fortresses, proving highly effective
at repelling invaders.

The extension of the fortress on the south side was achieved
by reclaiming land from the River Thames. This made Henry III's
main watergate, the Bloody Tower (then called the Garden Tower),
redundant because it was no longer on the river. It was therefore
replaced by a portcullis, and a new, wider riverside gate – St Thomas's
Tower – was built (fig. 53). This served as the entrance for prisoners
brought by river to the Tower to await their fate, and it later became
known as Traitors' Gate. It also fulfilled a more pleasant function,
though, because the King ordered a private suite of rooms above the
gate, linked to the Wakefield Tower by a bridge (fig. 54). These well-
appointed rooms included a tiny oratory, chambers, fireplaces and
latrines, and were decorated with painted statues and large stained-

*54. The Inmost Ward as
it might have looked in
1300. The royal palace,
to the south of the White
Tower, has been extended
by Edward I. The King's
accommodation included
a 'new hall and chamber'
over St Thomas's Tower,
shown at the bottom left
of the illustration.*

55. A reconstruction
of the Tower as it might
have looked c. 1300,
on the completion of
Edward I's works. The moat
is now filled with water and
encircles the entire fortress,
and the outer defences have
been greatly strengthened.
The basic form of the Tower
complex is the same today.

glass windows from which the King could watch his prisoners arriving
to meet their fate (figs. 48 and 51).

Meanwhile, Edward also reorganized the landward entrance to
the Tower, moving the main gate to the south-west corner. Visitors
would be confronted by a series of imposing towers and gateways.
A stone causeway from Tower Hill led to the Lion Tower, which was
surrounded by the new moat extension and defended by two gates
and a drawbridge. Beyond that were the twin-towered gateways of
the Middle and Byward towers, complete with drawbridges, gates
and portcullises (fig. 57). The King also added the gigantic Beauchamp
Tower to the western inner curtain wall in 1281 (fig. 56). Five years later,
he turned his attention to the Chapel of St Peter ad Vincula, which was
completely rebuilt.

Edward completed his improvements to the Tower in just eleven
years, from 1275 to 1286 (fig. 55). Speed came at a price, however: the

The Story of The Tower of London

works cost £21,000, more than twice the amount that his extravagant father had lavished on the fortress. But he did not wait for their completion before putting the Tower to full use.

By the 1270s England's Jewish population had become the subject of intense jealousy and resentment. As well as having made a profitable living in such financial services as moneylending, they were also suspected of 'clipping' the coinage – shaving metal from a coin's circumference, thus reducing its true value. This prompted the King to recall all of the nation's coinage in 1279 so that it could be recast in the Tower's newly established Mint (see pages 70–73).

There was a populous Jewish community in Cheapside, not far from the Tower. This was no accident of geography: the Jews had traditionally enjoyed royal protection, which had been exercised by the Constable of the Tower. But Edward I was less inclined than his predecessors to protect the Jews in his kingdom, because he had discovered a new source of loans: Italian bankers in Lombardy.

In 1278 Edward withdrew a number of the Jews' special privileges, and during the next two years he had no fewer than 600 of them rounded up and thrown into the Tower's dungeons (fig. 47). There were

56. (left) The Beauchamp Tower. This gigantic tower was built by Edward I in 1281 to strengthen the outer defences. It presented a deliberately imposing sight to the inhabitants of the city.

57. The Byward Tower, built by Edward I as part of a series of imposing towers and gateways that visitors had to pass through on entering the fortress. The modern-day visitor route is much as it was then.

so many Jewish prisoners that the cells could not accommodate them all, and many were crammed into the former elephant house of the Menagerie. Half of those arrested were eventually hanged on the charge of debasing the coinage. Those who survived were held as hostages, and their families were obliged to pay huge ransoms for their release. When a local judge, Henry de Bray, bravely spoke out against the injustice, he too was arrested. He broke away from his captors and, bound with cords, threw himself into the Thames, but was fished out and continued his journey to the Tower. He eventually succeeded in taking his life, thus becoming the Tower's first recorded suicide.

It is perhaps little wonder that during the reign of this warlike king, the Tower became the main repository for the Great Wardrobe's arms and armour. This was managed and augmented by workshops present there since at least 1273. An attempted theft at Westminster in 1303 prompted the transfer of the more valuable and precious-metal items from there to the Tower.

Edward was succeeded by his son, Edward II (1307–27). Lacking in any kingly qualities, Edward preferred the company of such male favourites as Piers Gaveston and Hugh Despenser, whom he endowed with great power, thus alienating his nobles and plunging the country into civil war once more.

One of the mightiest nobles to rebel against the Crown was Roger Mortimer, a Marcher lord with vast estates along the Welsh borders. Having surrendered to the King in January 1322, he was taken to the Tower for what looked set to be a lifelong imprisonment. The fortress in which he was incarcerated had changed little since the reign of Edward I. Apart from the reconstruction of the riverside wall between the Byward Tower and St Thomas's Tower in 1324, Edward II showed no interest in the fabric of the Tower. However, it was during his reign that there was significant growth in some of the functions and institutions that would dominate the fortress's later history – notably its role as keeper of state and legal records (see pages 58–59). By the 1320s record storage had already expanded into the White Tower chapel, and a system of proper sorting and filing was introduced.

Mortimer was not a man to live out his days in quiet contemplation of his misdeeds, and he soon began plotting with Edward's wife, Isabella, the so-called 'She-wolf of France' (fig. 58). Isabella was very familiar with the Tower, having endured a rather lonely existence there while her husband pursued his male favourites. It was said that she passed the time by reading romances from the Tower's library.

toff kemences en hollande z
zeellande · A moult grant

plente / Car moult trouuent
le pape ticke et bien pourueu

These may have inspired her to strike up an affair with Mortimer.
United by their contempt for the King and their hatred of his
favourites, as well as by a strong physical attraction, they resolved
upon seizing power. Taking advantage of the celebrations for the feast
day of St Peter ad Vincula, on 1 August 1323, Mortimer carried out a
daring escape plan, which involved digging himself out of his cell and
scaling the walls of the fortress with a rope ladder. He fled to France,
where he and his royal lover whipped up support for an invasion of
England. They returned in triumph in 1326, and early the following
year Edward was forced to abdicate. He was subsequently murdered
at Berkeley Castle, Gloucestershire.

Edward's son and successor, Edward III, had no liking for
Mortimer, whose arrogance and ambition made him dangerous
enemies among the nobility. The young King had him arrested
and thrown into the Tower in October 1330. This time, there would
be no escape. Mortimer was found guilty of treason and hanged
at Tyburn.

58. Isabella, the 'She-wolf of France', who rebelled against her husband, Edward II, with her lover, Roger Mortimer. Mortimer was one of only a handful of prisoners who succeeded in escaping from the Tower, but he was later re-incarcerated there by Isabella's son, Edward III.

In Focus
The Nation's Memory

Medieval government produced a vast volume of documents, including legal and diplomatic papers, charters, and grants of land and property. It was important to keep copies of these documents for future reference by government officials and lawyers, as well as to form a record of the reign of the presiding monarch. Most records were kept on sheets of parchment or paper rolled up for storage, which inspired the name of their official keeper, the Master of the Rolls.

For centuries, the monarch kept these documents with them wherever they travelled, but the growing volume forced the papers to be stored in a permanent – and very secure – space. From at least the late thirteenth century, the Tower became a major repository of these records, along with Westminster Abbey and, from the late fourteenth century, the court of Chancery in Chancery Lane. Purpose-built storage for the records was never provided at the fortress, so they competed for space with weapons, gunpowder, prisoners and even royalty. They were also frequently moved from place to place as other, more urgent demands took priority. Thus, in 1360 a collection of documents had to be moved from the White Tower in order to make way for the captured King of France. In the later Middle Ages, the main repository was in the Wakefield Tower, but by the reign of James I the White Tower was again in use.

Although of major political importance, the government documents housed at the Tower tended to take second place to the Ordnance, which is perhaps natural given the essentially military function of the fortress. But when William Prynne took over the custodianship of the records in 1660, he was appalled by the conditions in which they were kept (fig. 60). He claimed that the papers were in 'a deplorable pickle ... overspread with dust and cobwebs and eaten up with rust, cankers, moths, worms, in their over-much neglected cells'.

By now, most of the records were kept in the Wakefield Tower and a building attached to its east side, but space was extremely

Ex Libris Tabularii Publici in Turre LONDINENSI.

59. (above) A book plate used by the Tower Record Office, c. 1760.

60. William Prynne, Keeper of Tower Records to Charles II, had his ears cut off by Charles I for seditious writings. He had been appalled by the state of the records when he took over their custodianship in 1660, claiming that they were in 'a deplorable pickle'.

restricted. Even worse was the storage provided in the White Tower chapel, which Prynne's successor, Sir Algernon May, described in no less scornful terms. The presses, he said, were 'broke down & burnt by the Soldiers who did lye there and the Rolles and whatever they were of several natures thrown into one heap contayneing diverse cart Loads all mingled promiscuously together'.

The situation had become so dire by 1704 that a House of Lords committee organized a formal inspection. Having found most of the records lying 'in a confused heap', it ordered the installation of proper shelves and presses. By 1707 the chapel had been transformed into a 'noble repository' (fig. 61). A few years later, improvements were made to the facilities in the Wakefield Tower, when new shelves and presses were added, and openings for sash windows were cut into the old medieval walls to let in more light (fig. 62).

The remainder of the eighteenth century saw further enhancements to the record storage at the Tower (fig. 59). In 1736, after more than twenty years of negotiations with the Ordnance, an additional room on the top floor of the White Tower was secured.

By the dawn of the nineteenth century, the Tower's record-keeping facilities were much more fit for purpose. In 1808 two rooms at the top of the north-east turret of the White Tower were converted to record storage, and three years later all the rooms on the two upper floors were fitted with skylights.

Ironically, however, by this time the days of the Tower Record Office were already numbered. In 1800 a House of Commons Select Committee recommended that the various record repositories in and around London should be concentrated in one building. A few more years of debate followed, until in 1838 the Public Record Office Act was passed, which re-centralized control of the records under the Master of the Rolls and a Deputy Keeper. In 1851 work began on the building of a new central repository in Chancery Lane (the design of which echoed the record storage in the White Tower), and when this opened seven years later, all of the records were transferred from the Tower.

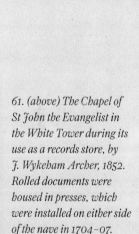

61. (above) The Chapel of St John the Evangelist in the White Tower during its use as a records store, by J. Wykeham Archer, 1852. Rolled documents were housed in presses, which were installed on either side of the nave in 1704–07.

62. The Record Office in the upper chamber of the Wakefield Tower, by Charles Tomkins, 1801. The panelling and cupboards that had been fitted early in the previous century can be seen.

Plague and Revolt

The history of the Tower in the fourteenth century was dominated by conflict at home and abroad. Even so, Edward III (1327–77) proved a far more capable ruler than his father had been, and his fifty-year reign witnessed the consolidation of royal power in England, as well as its extension across the Channel.

Edward had spent much of his childhood at the Tower, as a semi-prisoner of his mother, Queen Isabella, and her lover Roger Mortimer. Notwithstanding, he chose to spend his honeymoon there with Philippa of Hainault in 1328. Two years later, pregnant with their first child (Edward, the 'Black Prince'), Philippa rode in state from the Tower to her coronation at Westminster Abbey. She gave birth to her next child – a daughter, Blanche – in the Tower. This was only the second royal birth recorded at the fortress – the first being Edward III's sister, known as 'Joan of the Tower', who married David II of Scotland.

If he was not overly fond of it as a residence, Edward fully appreciated the Tower's defensive importance (fig. 64). In 1335 he therefore ordered a survey of its condition, conscious that the fortress had suffered both neglect and damage during his father's reign. He experienced the erosion of its defences first hand when he arrived unannounced one night in December 1340 and was able to gain entry without being challenged. The Constable, Sir Nicholas de la Beche, was dismissed and imprisoned for dereliction of duty, and Edward was inspired to carry out the necessary overhaul of security post-haste. He ordered the sheriffs of London to contribute £40 'to be spent about the Tower of London which is in great need of repair'.

63. (previous pages) A detail of a drawing of the White Tower in 1782, with the annex attributed to Edward III; see fig. 66.

64. (right) A portcullis at the Tower, showing the lowering mechanism. In 1336 Edward III ordered that the gates be locked from sunset to dawn, and that the officers and guards must stay inside the fortress at night.

65. (opposite) The Bloody Tower gate passage, showing the highly decorative vault inserted for Edward III c. 1362 by Robert Yevele, brother of Henry, one of the most famous architects of the Middle Ages. Watercolour by Frederick Nash, 1821.

Plague and Revolt

The resulting works included the strengthening of Edward's grandfather's defences, particularly the heightening of the southern curtain wall, which ran along the river, and the construction of a small watergate – the Cradle Tower – at its south-eastern corner. Another tower, the Develin, was also rebuilt near by, together with a new causeway to provide pedestrian access to St Katharine's Hospital, a religious community and hospital to the east founded by the wife of King Stephen in 1147.

Edward III did not entirely neglect the residential accommodation within the Tower, however. The Great Hall, to the south of the White Tower, was substantially altered in 1336–37, and the outmoded gables that had framed its north windows were replaced by a flat parapet. The King also ordered the Constable's lodgings to be rebuilt on the site now occupied by the Queen's House. Meanwhile, Henry III's watergate beside the Wakefield Tower was extended to form the basis of the existing Bloody Tower, and a beautiful vault was created over the gate passage (fig. 65).

Most of the other works to the Tower during Edward's reign were closely tied to the Hundred Years War between England and France, which formally began with the King's claiming the French throne in 1340 and ended with French victory in 1453 (fig. 67). The most important change that it inspired was the building of the Tower wharf, from where

67. Edward III arriving in France in 1346, during one of the campaigns of the Hundred Years War. The supplies that are being unloaded around him had been stored at the Tower of London. This was the beginning of the Tower's long history as the greatest arsenal in the country.

English troops could set sail for the Channel. The Tower was also increasingly used to make and store weapons and supplies – a function that continued to grow during the centuries that followed (see pages 128–35). As a result, by 1361 the headquarters of the Great Wardrobe had moved to new premises near Baynard's Castle, at the western end of the City of London. Meanwhile, the Privy Wardrobe assumed responsibility for military supplies, which competed for space with the King's jewels and crowns.

The role of the fortress as a prison also continued. Among the most notable inmates was Edward's brother-in-law David II, who had been captured at the Battle of Neville's Cross in 1346. It was not until eleven years later that he was released as part of the Treaty of Berwick, along with the promise of 100,000 marks in ransom by the Scots. Two years later, in 1359, the Tower welcomed another royal prisoner. The campaign of Edward III in France had gone from strength to strength during the previous two decades. He had won a spectacular victory at Crécy in 1346, and the triumph of his son, Edward the Black Prince, at Poitiers ten years later resulted in the capture of the French King, Jean II. Jean's

Plague and Revolt

68. A detail of a wall painting in the Byward Tower, which was rediscovered in 1953. The figures of St Michael (shown here) and St John the Baptist flank a Crucifixion scene. The painting probably dates from the turbulent years of Richard II's reign (1377–99).

imprisonment, along with his fourth son Philippe, was hardly onerous. He was kept in very comfortable lodgings in the White Tower, and the accounts for his first day of captivity there reveal that his household was allowed seventy-four loaves of bread, twenty-one gallons of wine, three sheep, one calf, twelve chickens and a capon. Jean and his son left the Tower the following year (perhaps somewhat reluctantly), after the conclusion of the Treaty of Brétigny.

On his death in 1377, Edward was succeeded by his grandson Richard II (1377–99), his son the Black Prince having died at Westminster Palace the previous year. The Tower formed an important backdrop from the very beginning of the new reign. It was here that Richard stayed before his coronation, according to what was now an established tradition, and from where he set out on the procession to Westminster Abbey, dressed all in white.

Although born of one of the greatest warriors of the age, Richard had more in common with the pious Henry III and the effeminate Edward II. He also shared their dangerous stubbornness. Richard inherited an impoverished and unstable country. His grandfather's wars had bankrupted the country and, together with the Black Death in 1348, had caused a severe manpower shortage. In a desperate attempt

The Story of The Tower of London

to raise money, the government had levied tax after tax on the declining population, resulting in deep-seated social ills.

The unrest came to a head in November 1380, when Parliament granted a new 'poll' tax requiring everyone over the age of fourteen, whether rich or poor, to pay one shilling to the Crown. This constituted a week's wages for a master craftsman and a month's wages for an agricultural labourer. When the tax collectors, who were universally despised, returned with only two thirds of the money, the Privy Council sent them back again in the spring of 1381. This prompted widespread resistance under the leadership of the charismatic Walter (or Wat) Tyler. He quickly amassed a huge body of supporters, and in June 1381 he marched on London with 20,000 men.

Along with his mother, Joan, the 'Fair Maid of Kent', King Richard had been hastily conveyed for his safety from Windsor to the Tower, where he was guarded by a garrison of 1000 men. On reaching the capital, the rebels headed straight for the fortress and quickly surrounded it. The King agreed to meet them, but as soon as the gates were opened to let him out, 400 rebels rushed in. Ransacking their way to the innermost parts of the fortress, they reached the first floor of the White Tower and burst into St John's Chapel, where they found the despised Archbishop of Canterbury, Simon Sudbury, leading some prayers. Without hesitation, they dragged him and his companions to Tower Hill and butchered them (fig. 70).

69. (left) The head of Simon Sudbury, who was dragged from St John's Chapel in the White Tower by participants of the Peasants' Revolt and butchered on Tower Hill. It took eight blows of the axe to sever his head.

70. The murder of Simon Sudbury as depicted in a fifteenth-century manuscript. The despised Archbishop of Canterbury was a target of the Peasants' Revolt, which was sparked by heavy taxation on a declining population.

71. The Peasants' Revolt of 1381, as depicted in Jean Froissart's Chronicles. *On the right, the young Richard II addresses the rebels at Mile End and offers terms. This peaceful encounter was followed by the bloodier events of the following day (shown on the left), when the King met the rebels again at Smithfield.*

It took eight blows of the amateur executioner's axe to sever the Archbishop's head, which was then set upon a pole on London Bridge (fig. 69).

Meanwhile (according to the contemporary chronicler Jean Froissart), inside the Tower the mob had ransacked the King's bedchamber and molested his mother and her ladies. Froissart described how the rebels 'arrogantly lay and sat and joked on the king's bed, whilst several asked the king's mother ... to kiss them'. Joan escaped with only a loss of dignity, but it had been a deeply shocking episode, illustrating the extent of the rebels' disdain for monarchical power. Steeled into more decisive action, Richard rode out to meet the rebels again and faced down their leader, Tyler, who was butchered by the King's men (fig. 71). Without his charismatic presence, the rebels lost the will to fight on and returned meekly to their homes.

The Story of The Tower of London

Richard's show of bravery had been fleeting and he soon reverted to the customary arrogance that had alienated swathes of his subjects. Six years after the Peasants' Revolt, it was the turn of his ministers to rebel against him. At Christmas 1387 Richard again sought refuge at the Tower as his enemies gathered their forces. Two years later, he ordered the final eastward extension of the wharf under the direction of the Clerk of Works, who was none other than the poet Geoffrey Chaucer. This created the south moat and sealed off the newly built Cradle Tower from the river. St Thomas's Tower remained accessible thanks to a bridged opening in the wharf.

The remainder of Richard II's reign was beset by troubles, and in September 1399 he was forced to sign an instrument of abdication at the Tower in favour of Henry of Bolingbroke, another grandson of Edward III (figs. 72 and 73). Within a fortnight, he was crowned Henry IV. Richard remained holed up at the Tower until a revolt in his name four months later prompted the new King to have him taken to Pontefract Castle in Yorkshire. By mid-February 1400, he was dead – of natural causes or by foul means, nobody knows.

72. Richard II arriving at the Tower as a prisoner in 1399. He was forced to sign an instrument of abdication soon afterwards in favour of Henry Bolingbroke, another grandson of Edward III.

73. Henry Bolingbroke entering London. His questionable claim to the throne meant that he was soon beset by plots to oust him from power. As a result, during the very earliest days of his reign, he was obliged to seek refuge in the Tower.

In Focus
The Mint

In around 1279 a new institution was founded at the Tower: the Mint. Before then, the minting of money had been carried out at a number of sites, including some workshops near St Paul's Cathedral. But Edward I was determined to keep the production of coins under closer control, given its immense importance to the nation's economy, so he moved the Mint to his London fortress.

The minting of coins was a rather different business from the usual activities at the Tower, and the Mint staff kept themselves separate from the rest of the community within the fortress. Security considerations also made their segregation necessary. The Mint workers literally held the wealth of the kingdom in their hands. The coinage also reinforced royal power in another important respect. In an age before mass communication, the vast majority of the monarch's subjects could gain an impression of what he or she looked like only from the coins that bore his or her likeness (fig. 75). Any tampering or forgery was therefore regarded as treason, and the punishments were severe.

For most of its existence at the Tower, the Mint was operated from a series of makeshift wooden sheds in the Outer Ward. The area in which these buildings were enclosed became known as Mint Street, and all of the 'incomings and outgoings' were closely guarded by the King's Porter. The Mint expanded over the centuries, along with the country's growing economy. Archaeological excavations revealed traces of its activity in the north-west bastion of the Tower, in the area that became Legge's Mount (fig. 76). By the sixteenth century, the Mint had spread along all three landward walls of the fortress.

74. (above) A shortage of silver prompted several crises during the Mint's history. In 1797, for example, the government was forced to circulate Spanish dollars, which were countermarked at the Mint with the head of George III.

75. The first gold sovereign was minted at the Tower in 1489. It was the largest gold coin that had been struck in England at that time.

Those who worked at the Mint endured hot, noisy and dangerous conditions. Machinery was not introduced until the seventeenth century, so for almost 400 years the coins were all produced by hand. The methods had changed little since Roman times. A handmade piece of metal was placed between engraved dies and struck with a hammer. Few workers emerged unscathed, and the loss of fingers or eyes was common.

The Mint workers had a particularly busy time during the reign of Henry VIII, when the dissolution of the monasteries led to an influx of silver that could be turned into coins. The French Ambassador reported that the workers of the Mint were obliged 'to coin money day and night' in order to keep up with the spendthrift King's urgent demand for cash. During the closing years of the reign, the coinage was debased so many times that all the nation's coins had to be re-minted. This prompted the construction of additional premises known as the Upper Mint, which was situated near the Salt Tower.

The pressure that the Great Debasement placed on the workers of the Mint is illustrated by the story of William Foxley, whose job was to make the melting pots. He fell asleep on the job in 1547, at the height of the pressure, and was said to have slept for fourteen days and fifteen nights before waking 'as if he had slept but one'.

Henry's daughter 'Bloody' Mary kept the coin makers just as busy. As part of her marriage settlement with Philip of Spain in May 1554, twenty cartloads of Spanish silver in ninety-seven chests were delivered to the Mint. By the following year, they had been re-minted into English coinage worth £17,600. Another recoinage during the reign of Mary's half-sister, Elizabeth I, prompted the rebuilding of the Upper Mint between 1560 and 1562.

The Mint continued to keep pace with demand until the middle of the seventeenth century, when the onset of the English Civil War caused a temporary disruption to service. The then Chief Engraver of the Mint, a fierce Royalist, abandoned his post to join King Charles I's court at Oxford, and took the Mint's dies with him. His foresight provided

76. Some of the Tudor metalworking vessels recovered from the excavation of the Mint building in Legge's Mount in 1976.

a much-needed boost to the Royalists, who were able to churn out coins without interruption. For all his scorn for the trappings of royalty, Oliver Cromwell made sure to have his likeness stamped on coins after he had ousted Charles from power. He was less willing to pay for the privilege, though: Thomas Simon, the new Chief Engraver of the Mint, complained to the Lord Protector 'that I and my servants have wrought five years without recompense'.

77. An engraving of 1750 showing a screw-operated coining press and dies. A blank disc of metal was placed on the die and pressed against an upper die by turning the screw. A rolling mill, used to produce sheet metal from which the blanks were cut, is being operated in the background. The new machines were a welcome development for the workers of the Mint, making the task both faster and less dangerous.

With the restoration of the monarchy in 1660 came the welcome introduction of machinery to the Mint, making the work much faster and less arduous. The new screw-operated presses could churn out an astonishing twenty to twenty-five coins per minute (fig. 77). Early in the reign, Samuel Pepys visited his friend Henry Slingsby, Deputy Master of the Mint, and was impressed by what he saw. He described the new machinery as 'so pretty that I did take note of every part of it', and enthused about the coins that it produced, which he said were 'some of the finest pieces of work, in embossed work, that ever I did see in my life, for fineness and smallness of the images thereon'. He concluded that 'the stamps of the new money ... are very neat and like the King'. Frances Stewart, one of the many court beauties with whom Charles II liked to surround himself, was allegedly the model for Britannia on the reverse of the coins – an image that lasted until 2008.

In 1696 the Mint received its most distinguished warden: the world-renowned scientist and mathematician Isaac Newton (fig. 78). His appointment came at a critical time. A severe shortage of silver – partly caused by the clipping of silver from the old hammered coins that had been minted before the introduction of machinery – had prompted an economic crisis. The Bank of England had been founded two years before and had lent the government £1.2 million in its first year, but this was not enough to fund King William III's war against France. Newton was therefore tasked with helping to solve this financial conundrum. The solution was a desperate one: the entire currency had to be returned to the Mint and reissued with milled edges to prevent clipping. Parliament was quick to agree to this, and Newton was appointed

Warden of the Mint in recognition of his services. He was promoted to the role of Master three years later and remained at the Mint until his death in 1727.

The recoinage organized by Newton prompted the creation of more space for the Mint. The workers had already started to take over some of the accommodation of the Tower garrison, causing the Lieutenant to complain that his soldiers were obliged to sleep three in a bed. The business of the Mint continued to outstrip the space available at the Tower, and by the end of the eighteenth century the government was obliged to find new accommodation (fig. 79). In 1798 the Privy Council decreed that the Mint should be rehoused outside the fortress, and by 1810 a new building had been erected for the purpose to the north-east of the Tower. But a link to its old home remained until 1843, thanks to a tunnel that ran from the new Mint to the Tower moat, from which water was drawn for the Mint's use. The new Mint continued to operate until 1968, when it was transferred to its current home in South Wales to prepare for decimalization.

78. The world-renowned scientist and mathematician Sir Isaac Newton, who was appointed Warden of the Mint in 1696. He was tasked with helping to resolve an economic crisis resulting from the debasement of the coinage.

79. An early nineteenth-century illustration of the Mint at the Tower, shortly before its departure to new premises. In the foreground is a screw-operated coining press, of the kind illustrated in fig. 77, with trays of finished coins either side.

The Wars of the Roses

The Tower continued to play a pivotal role in the nation's history during the fifteenth century – one of the most turbulent eras that the monarchy had ever known. The questionable claim of Henry IV (1399–1413) to the throne resulted in numerous plots and rebellions. At the very beginning of his reign, he was obliged to seek refuge in the London fortress when the late King Richard II's supporters staged a short-lived *coup d'état*.

Henry's relations with Scotland and Wales also proved troublesome, and the new King wasted no time in rounding up the ringleaders. The son and family of the Welsh patriot Owen Glendower were imprisoned in the Tower in 1408. They joined another Celtic inmate. Two years earlier, the young heir to the Scottish throne had been shipwrecked off the east coast of England. The eleven-year-old Prince James Stewart had been hastily (and illegally) conveyed to the Tower of London, where he remained for the next two years, before being moved to Nottingham Castle. News of his capture hastened the death of his father, Robert III, which meant that James became King of Scotland while a prisoner at the Tower. Only during the reign of Henry VI was James finally allowed to return to his native kingdom.

Other developments at the Tower indicate a renewed focus on its defensive function in these violent times. During the first decade of the fifteenth century, the Armoury was established as a separate body from the Wardrobe. The Keeper of the Privy Wardrobe ceased to appear in the accounts, and some of his functions were taken over by the 'Keeper of the King's Armour in the Tower'. This new institution survived, with its own staff and premises within the fortress, until the seventeenth century.

Henry V (1413–22) was chiselled from the same warrior stock as William the Conqueror and Edward I (fig. 82). On his father's death, he rode to the Tower with 'a great rout of lords and knights', and there created a new company of Knights of the Bath (fig. 81). But England did not long benefit from Henry's strong and capable leadership, for his sights were set on finally vanquishing the French. His ambitions would have a profound effect on the kingdom's greatest fortress.

Three months after his accession, Henry appointed an experienced fletcher named Nicholas Mynot as Keeper of the King's Arrows in the Tower Armoury. Mynot was charged with replenishing the store of arrows and longbows in the fortress in preparation for his royal master's campaign in France. It was the first step towards transforming the fortress into the headquarters for the war effort. The following year,

80. (previous pages) The Wakefield Tower oratory; see fig. 88.

81. As part of his inauguration into the Order of the Bath (established by Henry IV in 1399), a knight would be bathed in the White Tower. This event would take place two days before a coronation. Sixty knights were invested there prior to Anne Boleyn's coronation in 1533.

The Wars of the Roses

Nicholas Merbury was appointed 'Master of the Kings engines and guns and of the Ordnance'. This signalled both the importance that the new King placed on the Tower's military function, and the origins of the Ordnance as an independent body, separate from the Wardrobe. Its growing significance mirrored the increasing sophistication of artillery as the century progressed.

The newly crafted bows and arrows from the Tower were put to good use at Agincourt in 1415, when Henry V and his 'happy few' defeated a French army four times their size. As many as 1500 French prisoners were taken back to England and incarcerated in the Tower, including the French King's nephew Charles, Duke of Orléans (fig. 39).

During the second half of the fifteenth century, the focus shifted from the Continent to home-grown conflict, when the so-called Wars of the Roses tore the country apart. The battles between the descendants of Edward III's sons Edmund, Duke of York (Yorkists), and John of Gaunt, Duke of Lancaster (Lancastrians), raged for thirty years, from 1455 until the Lancastrian Henry Tudor's triumph at the Battle of Bosworth in 1485.

The Tower saw its first action in the conflict in 1460 when it was held for Henry VI (1422–61; 1470–71) against the Yorkists, who had captured the King at Northampton in July that year (fig. 84). Under siege from a

formidable army of Londoners, a desperate Lord Scales, Constable of the Tower, 'cast wild fire into the city, and shot in small guns ... and hurt men and women and children in the streets', while the citizens 'laid great bombards [cannon] on the far side of the Thames ... and crazed the walls thereof in divers places' (fig. 83). With no hope of relief, Scales eventually surrendered on 19 July.

Three months after the Duke of York's death at the Battle of Wakefield in December 1460, his son won a resounding victory at Towton, forcing the King into hiding and claiming the Crown for himself as Edward IV (1461–70; 1471–83; fig. 85). Henry was captured in 1465 and brought 'as a traitor and criminal to London, and imprisoned in the Tower there; where, like a true follower of Christ, he patiently endured hunger, thirst, mockings, derisions, abuse and many other hardships'. Henry remained there until 1470, when Edward was temporarily overthrown, but the Yorkist King returned in triumph in 1471.

Edward immediately ordered reinforcements to the Tower, particularly along the wharf, where earthworks were hastily erected and makeshift gun emplacements fashioned out of earth-filled barrels. These enabled him to hold off his enemies in the capital,

84. Henry VI, who was deposed by Edward IV in 1461 and later imprisoned in the Tower. Legend has it that he was murdered while at prayer in the Wakefield Tower.

85. The handsome and charismatic Yorkist king Edward IV, who claimed the throne after winning a resounding victory against the Lancastrians at Towton in 1461. His brother George, Duke of Clarence, and his two young sons, Edward and Richard, all met their deaths at the Tower.

The Wars of the Roses

86. The Yorkists defeat the Lancastrians at the Battle of Tewkesbury in 1471. The encounter would prove decisive, at last putting an end to Margaret of Anjou's campaign against Edward IV.

87. Margaret of Anjou in a dungeon with a demon, from the Hours of Jeanne de Bourbon, c. 1475. The vanquished wife of Henry VI was brought to the Tower straight after Tewkesbury. It was rumoured that her husband was put to death on the very night of her arrival.

and shortly afterwards he finally vanquished Henry's wife, the formidable Margaret of Anjou, and her allies at the battles of Barnet and Tewkesbury (fig. 86). Margaret was brought to the Tower, where Henry VI was already a prisoner. But Margaret never saw her husband again: on the very night of her arrival, Henry died (fig. 87). Legend has it that the former King was murdered while at prayer in the oratory of the Wakefield Tower (fig. 88). Richard, Duke of Gloucester, brother of the King, was in charge of the Tower that night, and a contemporary claimed that Henry had been 'stykked with a dagger' wielded by him.

Margaret of Anjou was inconsolable on learning of her husband's death some days later, and it was said that her cries of lament could be heard by people in the nearby streets. She was released from the Tower soon afterwards and eventually allowed to return to her native France.

For the remainder of his reign, Edward battled to remove all opponents to the Yorkist regime – including his own brother, George, Duke of Clarence. Ambitious, volatile and increasingly paranoid,

Clarence was forever plotting against his elder brother. In 1476 Clarence's personal astronomer was arrested and placed in the Tower, and under torture confessed that he had used the black arts to try to bring about the King's death. Edward subsequently accused his brother of treason and had him thrown into the Tower. Having been found guilty, Clarence was put to death there in February 1478 – legend has it by being drowned in a butt of Malmsey wine (fig. 89).

The final years of Edward's reign saw the last extension of the Tower's fortified area. An enclosure was created at the south end of Tower Hill to protect the western entrance – the first part of the fortress designed to carry and resist gunfire. A new official was appointed to guard this important outpost. In March 1484 Thomas Redhede became Porter of the Tower of London and Keeper of 'le Bulwark', as it became known. The job came with a house inside the enclosure, and the enterprising Redhede later made a profitable, if illegal, business of subletting houses to his neighbours.

At around the same time, the south side of the Byward Tower was fortified with the building of the existing triangular-shaped turret, equipped with loopholes for small cannon and handguns. This was an innovative piece of defensive architecture, and one of the earliest examples that can be found.

Edward may have strengthened the Tower against external threats, but one of the darkest deeds in its turbulent history would be committed against his own flesh and blood within its apparently safe confines (see pages 82–83).

88. (above) The Wakefield Tower oratory was originally built by Henry III as part of a luxurious suite of royal apartments.

89. Legend has it that Edward IV's rebellious brother George, Duke of Clarence, was executed in the Bowyer Tower in 1478 by drowning in a butt of Malmsey wine. One of Clarence's retainers had confessed under torture at the Tower that his master had 'imagined and compassed' the death of the King.

In Focus
The Princes in the Tower

90. (above) Edward V and his younger brother Richard, known as the 'Princes in the Tower', after Paul Delaroche, 1831. The skeletons of two young boys were discovered in 1674 during the demolition of the old royal palace next to the White Tower.

91. The murder of the Princes in the Tower as imagined by the painter James Northcote, c. 1790. Their disappearance in 1483 has proved one of the most controversial events in the Tower's history, sparking endless debate among historians.

Henry VI's was not the only alleged murder to be placed at the door of Richard, Duke of Gloucester. On the death of his brother in 1483, the Duke became Lord Protector of Edward's son and heir, the twelve-year-old King Edward V. He wasted no time in placing the boy in the Tower, ostensibly for his protection, but in reality to fortify his own increasingly vulnerable position. Having proclaimed himself King, Richard soon amassed a dangerous body of enemies at court (fig. 92). His increasing paranoia led to his having an ally, Lord Hastings, arrested during a council meeting at the Tower in June 1483 and summarily executed.

That same month, Edward and his younger brother Richard, who had joined him at the Tower, were seen for the final time (fig. 90). The last reference to them is in the *Great Chronicle*, which on 16 June records that 'the children of King Edward' were 'seen shooting [arrows] and playing in the garden of the Tower sundry times'. According to the Italian chronicler Dominic Mancini, soon afterwards the boys were 'withdrawn to the inner apartments of the Tower proper, and day by day began to be seen more rarely behind the bars and windows'. This suggests that Richard had moved them from the Garden or 'Bloody' Tower to the White Tower, where royal captives tended to be held. Other chroniclers concur that the boys were 'holden more straight' from that time onwards.

What happened next has been the subject of intense debate ever since, and is one of the darkest chapters in the Tower's long history. It is now widely accepted that some time during the autumn of 1483 the two princes were quietly murdered (fig. 91). At whose hands, it will probably never be known. Richard III, who had invalidated his nephews' claim to the throne and had himself crowned King in July, has long been the prime suspect, but there were others with a vested interest in getting the boys out of the way – not least Richard's successor, Henry VII.

The two princes had apparently disappeared without trace, but in 1674 a remarkable discovery was made at the Tower. The then King, Charles II, ordered the demolition of what remained of the royal palace to the south of the White Tower, including a turret that had once contained a privy staircase leading into St John's Chapel. Beneath the foundations of the staircase, some 3 metres (10 ft) below the ground, the workmen were astonished to find a wooden chest containing two skeletons (fig. 93). They were clearly the bones of children, and their height coincided with the age of the two princes when they disappeared. Moreover, an eyewitness described 'pieces of rag and velvet' that adhered to the bones – the latter material being the exclusive preserve of royalty and nobility. The same witness was in no doubt about the identity of the skeletons: 'This day I ... saw working men dig out of a stairway in the White Tower the bones of those two Princes who were foully murdered by Richard III.'

The skeletons became something of a tourist attraction and

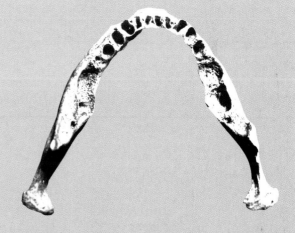

remained on display for the next four years, until Charles II arranged for their reburial in Westminster Abbey. They lie there still, with a brief interruption in 1933, when a re-examination provided compelling evidence that they were the two princes. The controversy surrounding their death shows no sign of abating.

92. (left) Richard III, who deposed his young nephew Edward V in 1483 and became the prime suspect in the murder of the princes. His role in their disappearance still divides opinion today.

93. The lower jaw of one of the two skeletons unearthed at the Tower in 1674. The skeletons were re-examined in 1933 and proved to be of two boys aged about twelve and ten – exactly the same ages as the princes when they disappeared.

The Tudors and the Tower

No other dynasty is as synonymous with the Tower's story as the Tudors. This was the era when more high-profile statesmen, churchmen and even queens went to the block than at any other time in its history (see pages 102–105). The fortress came to epitomize the brutality of the Tudor regime and of its most famous king, Henry VIII.

Henry's father, Henry VII (1485–1509), became the first Tudor king when he triumphed over Richard III at the Battle of Bosworth. His rather tenuous claim ensured that he and his descendants would never feel secure on the throne, and many of the prisoners in the Tower during the Tudor era were rival claimants. They included Edward, Earl of Warwick, the ten-year-old son of Edward IV's brother George, Duke of Clarence. Very soon after his accession, Henry had the boy brought to the Tower, where he was kept under strict surveillance. In 1497 he was joined by the 'Pretender' Perkin Warbeck, who claimed to be Richard, Duke of York, one of the two sons of Edward IV who had disappeared in the Tower fourteen years earlier. The wily King ensured that Warwick and Warbeck were given cells adjacent to each other and were allowed to converse regularly. During the two years that followed, he set spies to watch for any sign of a conspiracy. Although there is no reliable evidence that the two young men were plotting against Henry, he had them accused of treason and executed in 1499.

Despite the brutal dispatch of his perceived rivals, Henry remained insecure on his throne. It may have been during his reign that the Yeomen of the Guard were formed. The official royal bodyguards, of which the Yeoman Warders were a detachment, were certainly well established by the time of his death in 1509. Their distinctive scarlet Tudor livery has been carried down through the centuries. It is thought that their nickname – 'Beefeaters' – derives from the fact that they were permitted to eat as much beef as they wanted from the King's table.

Henry VII used the Tower as a home, not just as a fortress – although he was the last monarch to do so. When his eldest son and heir, Arthur, married Katherine of Aragon, daughter of Ferdinand and Isabella of Spain, the famously parsimonious King splashed out on lavish new royal apartments in the Lanthorn and Cradle towers. He also commissioned work on a new tower and, later, a new garden in the fashionable Renaissance style.

But the fifteen-year-old groom died just five months after the wedding, and Henry's beloved wife, Elizabeth of York, followed their son to the grave less than a year later (fig. 96). She had just given birth to a daughter, Katherine, in the Tower and probably developed puerperal

94. (previous pages) The Meeting of Sir Thomas More with his Daughter after his Sentence of Death *by William Frederick Yeames, 1863; see fig. 101.*

95. Henry VIII by Joos van Cleve, c. 1535. Henry's 'reign of terror' saw more victims imprisoned, tortured and executed at the Tower than at any other time in its history.

The Story of The Tower of London

MARCI 10
TE IN MVDVM VNIVERSV ET ADICAT
EVANGELIVM OMNI CREATVR

The Tudors and the Tower

96. Henry VII married Elizabeth of York the year after becoming King in order to cement the tenuous alliance between the Yorkists and the Lancastrians. Elizabeth died at the Tower in February 1503, after giving birth to a short-lived daughter.

fever. The baby died before her mother. A grief-stricken Henry gave orders for his wife's body to be embalmed, and it lay in state for three days in St John's Chapel in the White Tower.

Henry was succeeded by his second son and namesake, a gloriously handsome, athletic and accomplished Renaissance prince who was as different from his grasping, paranoid father as it was possible to be (fig. 95). Within hours of succeeding to the throne, Henry VIII (1509–47) made a dramatic and symbolic gesture to distance himself from the unpopular regime of his predecessor. He had his father's despised councillors Richard Empson and Edmund Dudley thrown into the Tower on trumped-up charges of treason. They were executed sixteen months later.

This set the tone for the remainder of Henry VIII's reign. After refurbishing the Tower for the joint coronation of himself and his late brother's widow, Katherine of Aragon, whom he had married soon after his accession, and rebuilding the Chapel of St Peter ad Vincula, which had burned down in 1512 (fig. 97), Henry virtually abandoned it as a residence and made it a place synonymous with terror, torture and death. As the contemporary chronicler Raphael Holinshed observed, the fortress became more 'an armourie and house of munition, and thereunto a place for the safekeeping of offenders than a palace roiall for a king or queen to sojourne in'.

Having inherited his father's fear of rival claimants, Henry used the fortress to eliminate some of the last scions of the House of York. They included William de la Pole, who was imprisoned in the Tower for thirty-eight years, for no other reason than that he had Yorkist blood coursing through his veins. His elder brother Edmund, Earl of Suffolk,

joined him there for a while, but was executed on Tower Hill in
April 1513.

Henry's insecurity intensified when his wife failed to produce
the male heir that was so vital to the stability of any ruling dynasty.
Convincing himself that God was displeased with him for marrying
his late brother's wife, Henry sought a divorce. His shrewd minister
Thomas Cromwell – then a rising star at the Tudor court – secured
this for him and in the process set in train a revolution in religion and
politics that would shake England to its core. Now Henry, not the Pope,
was head of the English Church.

Cromwell was richly rewarded for his pains. Among his many
other appointments was that of Master of the Jewels, which made him
a regular visitor to the Tower. He wasted no time in initiating a survey

*97. The interior of the
Chapel of St Peter ad
Vincula. Originally a
parish church lying outside
the fortress, it was brought
within the complex by the
gradual extension of the
Tower's defences during the
twelfth century. The chapel
has recently been restored.*

of the fortress. The findings did not make pleasant reading. Virtually every tower and intervening stretch of wall required attention. The repairs would cost £3593 4s. 1d (equivalent to more than £1 million today) and involve 2937 tons of Caen stone. Perhaps corners were cut in the ensuing works, which were under way by 1532, because the defences still fell short of the standards of the time. Rather than installing the low, angular bastions that were needed to carry and resist artillery, timber platforms were placed on three of the towers along the northern curtain wall, and in two positions over the Mint, on St Thomas's Tower and on top of the White Tower.

More care was taken over improving the facilities for the Wardrobe. During the Middle Ages, the main repository may have been housed in an annex adjoining the east side of the White Tower (fig. 66). In 1532, however, a new storehouse was created that stretched between the Broad Arrow and Wardrobe towers. This new accommodation was justified, for the contents of the Wardrobe had grown considerably during Henry's reign. An

The Story of The Tower of London

inventory taken at the time of his death in 1547 shows that it contained numerous beds, chairs, canopies, carpets and cushions, as well as more than 150 tapestries and wall hangings. Many of these items were fashioned from luxurious fabrics, such as silver and gold cloth, velvet and damask, and some were embellished with precious stones.

Shortly after the Wardrobe moved to its new accommodation, Henry set about preparing the Tower for the coronation of his new Queen, Anne Boleyn, in June 1533 (fig. 98). He ordered the refurbishment of the Great Watching Chamber (his guardroom) and Privy Chamber (his bedroom). At the same time, the Great Chamber within the Queen's own apartments was given a new roof and floor. A reference to 'Antyk' work suggests that the decoration may have included classical motifs – a theme that was continued in Anne's elaborate coronation procession. Henry VIII's Great Hall was also repaired and redecorated in preparation for the coronation celebrations, and the kitchens were overhauled in time for the sumptuous feasting. Finally, the royal lodgings over St Thomas's Tower were largely rebuilt to accommodate the King's chief household officers (fig. 99). At the same time, onion domes were added to the top of the White Tower, creating the iconic silhouette that is still recognized the world over (fig. 100). Thus embellished, the fortress played its part magnificently in the lavish ceremonials. But thereafter, Henry rarely – if ever – stayed there again. The Tower resumed its role as a place of terror once more.

Several high-profile opponents to the King's new marriage and the subsequent religious reforms found themselves holed up in

98. (opposite) A row of seven timber-framed 'houses of offices' was erected to the north of the Wakefield Tower in 1533. This view by G.R. Gill was made shortly before the buildings were taken down in 1846.

99. A view of the Tower in 1544. The royal lodgings are to the front and right of the White Tower. Those with larger windows denote rooms added or refurbished under Henry VII and Henry VIII. Tower Hill, with its scaffold, is to the upper left of the fortress.

100. *Henry VIII commissioned the onion domes on the roof of the White Tower as part of the improvements to the fortress in preparation for Anne Boleyn's coronation in 1533.*

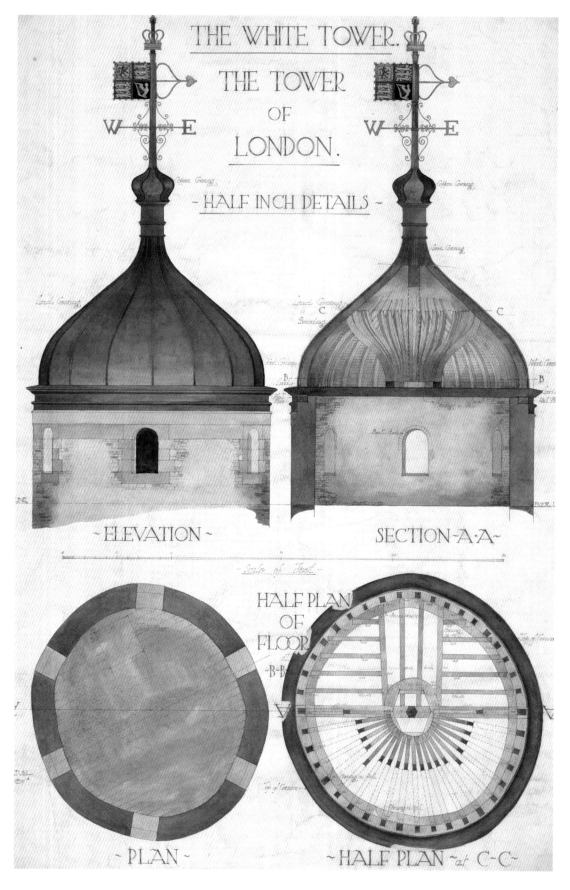

the fortress – most famously his former Lord Chancellor Thomas More (fig. 101). Having refused to take the oath recognizing Henry as Supreme Head of the Church, in April 1534 More was taken by river from his home in Chelsea to the Tower, where he was confined to the cold, damp cell at the bottom of the Bell Tower. His co-objector, the aged Bishop John Fisher, was imprisoned in the cell above on the same charges. Although More was at first permitted some comforts, such as daily walks in the Tower gardens, as he continued to resist pressure to conform, his privileges were gradually withdrawn. He passed his miserable hours of confinement in writing long religious treatises (which were among many literary works conceived by prisoners in the Tower), but grew weary of life, confessing to a fellow prisoner: 'I have since I came to the Tower looked once or twice to have given up my ghost before this.' His suffering came to an end in July 1535, when he was executed on Tower Hill, two weeks after Fisher.

Henry VIII sent more men and women to their deaths than any other monarch, and during the last ten years of his reign the Tower was crowded with the terrified subjects who had been imprisoned on his orders. The King did not flinch from putting even those closest to him to the axe – or, in the case of his once adored second wife, Anne Boleyn, to the sword. His fourth wife, Catherine Howard, was also executed at the Tower on charges of adultery – although in her case, the charges were probably justified. Henry did at least ensure that his victims were comfortably housed as they awaited their deaths. In 1540 he agreed that new lodgings (today known as the Queen's House) could be built for the Lieutenant of the Tower and his highest-ranking prisoners. Situated on the south-west corner of Tower Green, these form the most

101. Sir Thomas More was imprisoned in the Bell Tower in 1534 after refusing to acknowledge Henry VIII's supremacy over the Church. He was executed on Tower Hill the following year. Here, he is shown saying farewell to his daughter in a painting by William Frederick Yeames, 1863.

complete timber-framed buildings in London from before the Great Fire in 1666 (fig. 102).

Meanwhile, Henry turned his attention to the remaining Yorkists in his realm. The aged Margaret Pole, daughter of Edward IV's brother George, Duke of Clarence, was incarcerated in the Tower in the autumn of 1539 (fig. 103). She was to spend almost two years there, until Henry decided to put to death all state prisoners held at the Tower. The Countess was woken early on the morning of 27 May 1541 and told to prepare for the end. There had been no time to build a scaffold, so only a scattering of straw marked the spot on Tower Green where she was to be beheaded. Although initially composed, when Margaret was told to place her head on the block, her self-control deserted her and she tried to escape. Her captors were forced to pinion her to the block, where the amateur executioner hacked at the poor woman's head and neck, eventually severing them after the eleventh blow.

The last high-profile Tower prisoner to be executed in this long and bloody reign was Henry Howard, Earl of Surrey. A gifted poet, Surrey was also highly volatile and a notorious drunk, whom the King called a 'foolish, proud boy'. He made a dangerous enemy of the late Queen Jane Seymour's brother, Edward, who was a dominant force at court. Edward played on the King's increasing paranoia and convinced him that the Howards were plotting to place Surrey on the throne when Henry died. The fact that Surrey had displayed royal arms on his coat of arms was evidence enough for the King, who ordered his arrest. Once in the Tower, Surrey hatched a daring plan to escape, which involved squeezing through the shaft that ran from the latrine into

102. (above) Tower Green in 1720. It was here that a number of notable prisoners were executed. Being put to death within the relative privacy of the Tower complex was a privilege extended to high-ranking prisoners. Most other prisoners were hauled to nearby Tower Hill, where the crowds could gather to enjoy the spectacle.

103. The execution of Margaret Pole, Countess of Salisbury, at the Tower in 1541 was one of the most horrific in the brutal history of the fortress. It took eleven blows of the axe to sever her head.

The Story of The Tower of London

the river below. He almost succeeded, but the guards raised the alarm when they saw that his bed was empty and found him making his way down the shaft. The hapless Earl was executed on Tower Hill on 19 January 1547. Just nine days later, Henry VIII breathed his last.

Henry's nine year-old son, Edward VI (1547–53) succeeded as King, under the protectorship of his uncle, Edward Seymour, Duke of Somerset. The pair rode in great state to the Tower three days after the old King's death and remained there for two weeks as preparations were made for Henry's funeral at Windsor, and – soon afterwards – Edward's coronation at Westminster Abbey (fig. 104).

A deadly rivalry soon sprang up between Protector Seymour and John Dudley, Earl of Warwick. Edward Seymour's position was rendered increasingly unstable by the behaviour of his volatile and ambitious brother Thomas, who recklessly attempted to kidnap the King in January 1549. Thomas Seymour was immediately arrested and taken to the Tower. He was found guilty of treason shortly afterwards and his own brother was obliged to sign the death warrant. Three years later, Edward Seymour himself, having been ousted by Dudley, faced the executioner's axe on Tower Hill.

Edward VI's brief reign came to a premature end on 6 July 1553, when he succumbed to a lingering illness that had been exacerbated by the ministrations of his physicians. Anxious to prevent the accession of Edward's staunchly Roman Catholic sister Mary, the Protestant Dudley orchestrated a coup by marrying his own son Guildford to Lady Jane Grey, the great-niece of Henry VIII, and placing her on the throne. Two

104. Edward VI's coronation procession from the Tower to Westminster, which took place on 20 February 1547. The young King had stayed at the fortress during the first two weeks of his reign while preparations were made for his father Henry VIII's funeral and his own coronation shortly afterwards.

105. Cranmer, at
the Traitor's Gate
*by Frederick Goodall,
1856. Thomas Cranmer,
the former Archbishop
of Canterbury, was
imprisoned at the Tower
in 1553–54. He was one of
many high-profile 'heretics'
to be burned during
'Bloody' Mary Tudor's
attempts to restore England
to the Roman Catholic fold.*

days after Edward's death, Jane (then aged sixteen or seventeen at most) was proclaimed Queen and entered the Tower with great ceremony – and reluctance. She would reign for just nine days. For all her faults, Mary was a true Tudor princess and wasted no time in rallying thousands of subjects to her cause. Soon, the Privy Council turned its coat and declared for Mary I (1553–58). On 19 July she was proclaimed Queen, to the great rejoicing of Londoners.

Meanwhile, England's shortest-reigning queen, Lady Jane, remained at the Tower. But it was now her fortress, not her palace. Mary arrived there on 3 August and immediately released the Catholic prisoners from her father's reign (fig. 105). Jane was kept in some comfort before her trial in November, when she and her husband were convicted of treason. But Mary bore her no ill-will, and it was rumoured that she would pardon her. A series of uprisings at the beginning of 1554 changed all of that. Jane's father had joined the plot to oust Mary – whose staunch Roman Catholicism and proposed marriage to Philip of Spain had rendered her deeply unpopular – from the throne. Mary reluctantly acknowledged that Jane was too dangerous a threat to be

The Story of The Tower of London

allowed to live. She was led to her execution on 12 February, having watched the headless body of her husband, Guildford Dudley, being carried back from Tower Hill.

Jane herself was afforded the privilege of a private execution within the Tower grounds. She remained calm as she walked to the scaffold, and in her final speech she expressed regret that she had allowed herself to be made Queen. She then asked the executioner to ensure a swift death and tied a blindfold over her eyes. But as she groped blindly for the block, panic overcame her and she cried, 'What shall I do? Where is it?' Someone stepped in to help, and Jane laid her head on the block. As she spoke her last words: 'Lord, into thy hands I commend my spirit', the axe fell (fig. 106).

It may have been a growing awareness of her unpopularity that prompted Mary, in 1555, to issue instructions to the Constable of the Tower that there should be no fewer than twenty-one 'discreet, trusty and personable yeomen of middle age', none 'above fifty or below thirty'. Seven were appointed Chief Yeoman Warders and given comfortable lodgings and good wages. The rest fared less well. In 1598

106. The Execution of Lady Jane Grey by Paul Delaroche, 1833. The 'nine days queen' succeeded Edward VI in 1553, but was swiftly deposed by the rightful heir, Mary Tudor.

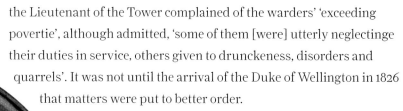

the Lieutenant of the Tower complained of the warders' 'exceeding povertie', although admitted, 'some of them [were] utterly neglectinge their duties in service, others given to drunckeness, disorders and quarrels'. It was not until the arrival of the Duke of Wellington in 1826 that matters were put to better order.

Mary also decreed that nine men from the ranks of the Yeoman Warders were to patrol during the day, and six at night. Detailed instructions were also set down for securing the keys at night. The original text provides an account of what has become known as the Ceremony of the Keys, which has been performed every night since:

And it is ordered that there shall be a place appointed under Locke and key where in the keys of the gates of the saide Tower shall be laide in the sight of the constable, the porter and two of the Yeoman Warders, or three of them at the least, and by two or three of them to be taken out when the[y] shall be occupied. And the key of that locke or coffer where the keys be, to be kepte by the porter or, in his absence, by the chiefe yeoman warder.

On Mary's death in November 1558, the throne passed to her younger half-sister, Elizabeth I (1558–1603), who entered the Tower to a rapturous reception on 28 November. Quite what she felt on returning to the fortress where she had been held prisoner during her half-sister's reign (see page 105) and where her mother, Anne Boleyn, had met her death can be only imagined. But statecraft overcame any sensibilities, and Elizabeth remained there with her council for several weeks to decide the future course of policy.

Although she had become Queen on a wave of popular rejoicing, it was not long before Elizabeth was under threat from rival claimants to the throne. Her refusal to marry and produce an heir made this threat all the more intense. Among her most dangerous rivals was Catherine Grey, sister of the ill-fated Jane (fig. 107). In 1560 the beautiful but naïve Catherine took the reckless step of marrying Edward Seymour, Earl of Hertford, son of the former Lord Protector. For a person of royal blood to marry without the monarch's consent was deemed treason, and Elizabeth wasted no time in placing Catherine (who was already pregnant) and Edward in the Tower.

In September 1561 Catherine was delivered of a son. The boy was christened in the Chapel of St Peter ad Vincula, under the flagstones of which lay his aunt. The birth of a male heir to her despised rival

107. Lady Catherine Grey, a rival to Elizabeth I, who imprisoned her in the Tower in 1561 for marrying without the Queen's permission. Catherine gave birth to her first child, Edward (shown here), during her imprisonment.

The Story of The Tower of London

intensified Elizabeth's fury, and she ordered that Catherine and her husband be kept strictly apart. But their gaolers took pity on them and allowed Seymour at least one conjugal visit to his wife. As a result, Catherine gave birth to a second son at the Tower in February 1563. The couple had obviously established quite a cosy fraternity within their prison, for the godfathers at this latest christening were two warders of the Tower.

The Queen's fury knew no bounds. The Spanish Ambassador observed that she turned 'the colour of a corpse' on hearing the news. She ordered that Catherine and Hertford be removed from the Tower and sent to different places of imprisonment, many miles apart. Heartbroken at being kept from her beloved husband, Catherine went on hunger strike and died in January 1568, aged just twenty-seven.

Elizabeth had rid herself of one rival, but there was another – far more dangerous – waiting in the wings. Mary, Queen of Scots, had a strong blood claim to the English throne, being the great-niece of Henry VIII (fig. 108). Although she became Elizabeth's prisoner in 1568, she could draw on the considerable body of Catholic supporters both in England and abroad. Numerous plots soon sprang up around her, all aiming to kill the English Queen and place her Scottish cousin on the throne. The Tower housed many of these plotters during the nineteen years of Mary's imprisonment, and the elaborate graffiti of those who were captured and incarcerated in the Beauchamp Tower can still be seen today (fig. 111). They included members of the notorious Babington Conspiracy, which led to Mary's own execution in 1587.

The closing years of Elizabeth's reign saw a growing number of prisoners in the Tower, as the increasingly suspicious Queen and her ever-vigilant ministers seized on any threat to her regime. They included the handsome young courtier Robert Devereux, Earl of Essex. He was thirty years younger than the Queen but paid court to her like a lover; however, in 1599 he overreached himself by defying her express command to quell a rebellion in Ireland and instead returned home in disgrace, having concluded a humiliating truce. In

108. Elizabeth I's most dangerous rival, Mary, Queen of Scots, fled to England in 1568 and immediately became the focus of plots and rebellions. The Babington Conspiracy of 1586 provided Elizabeth's spymaster, Sir Francis Walsingham, with enough evidence to seal Mary's doom. The conspirators were thrown into the Tower and suffered traitors' deaths.

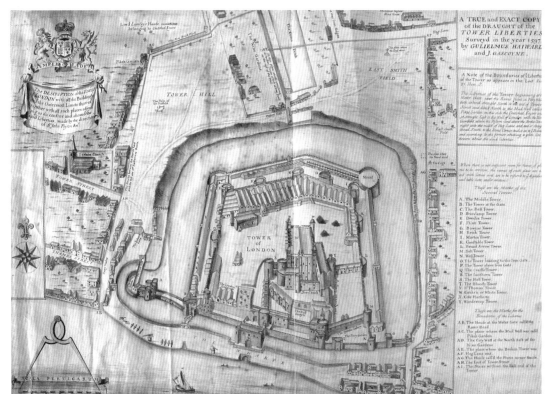

109. A plan of the Tower prepared c. 1597 to accompany a report on its condition. The earliest measured plan of the fortress, it is the only detailed record of many of the medieval and Tudor buildings that were swept away or drastically modified in the seventeenth century, notably the royal lodgings and Great Hall to the south of the White Tower.

desperation, Essex gathered together a body of supporters, including his close friend Henry Wriothesley, Earl of Southampton, and in 1601 launched a badly organized revolt against Elizabeth and her council. This soon ended in ignominious defeat, and Essex and Southampton were conveyed to the Tower, along with eighty of their followers. A verdict of treason was swiftly passed, and Essex awaited his fate in the Devereux Tower.

Legend has it that the disgraced Earl made one last attempt to regain his royal mistress's favour. It was said that in happier days, Elizabeth had given him a ring, assuring him that if ever he returned it, he would be forgiven, no matter what his crime. Leaning out of the Devereux Tower, Essex saw a pageboy passing by and threw the ring to him, begging him to take it to Lady Scrope, a friend of his at court. But instead, the boy gave it to Lady Nottingham, the wife of one of Essex's fiercest enemies. Realizing its significance, Lady Nottingham hid the ring away, determined that the Queen would never know of it.

Having received no reprieve, Essex went to his death on 25 February 1601. He had at least been afforded the privilege of a private execution within the Tower's walls – although the axeman botched the job and it took three blows to sever the Earl's head. Two years later, so the story goes, Lady Nottingham confessed her secret to Elizabeth as both women were close to death. The anguished Queen cried: 'God may forgive you – but I never can.'

Elizabeth had at least spared Essex's companion, the charismatic Earl of Southampton. He remained a prisoner in the Tower for the rest of her reign, but was housed in a comfortable apartment in the royal palace. He was allowed to keep his beloved cat for company, and the

The Story of The Tower of London

animal features in a portrait of the Earl that he had painted during his imprisonment (fig. 110).

Although she sent many men (and women) to the Tower during her long reign, Elizabeth followed the examples of her predecessors and neglected it as a residence. Like her father, though, she considerably enhanced the contents of the Wardrobe. A visitor to the Tower in 1598 was shown 'an immense quantity of bed-furniture, such as canopies; and the like, some of them most richly ornamented with pearl, some royal dresses so extremely magnificent, as to raise any one's admiration at the sums they must have cost'. Another foreign visitor, Baron Waldstein, was similarly impressed two years later, as he described the 'sixty tapestries very richly and splendidly worked with gold thread ... and numerous chairs which had their cushions woven in silk and gold thread'.

Elizabeth also commissioned a report on the condition of the Tower in 1597, and it is thanks to the detailed plan it contained that we know so much about the layout of the fortress at the end of the Tudor era (fig. 109). But the Queen chose not to commission the repairs that were so obviously needed; understandably, perhaps, she had never shown any inclination to stay at the Tower, except when tradition required it at the beginning of her reign. By the time of her death in 1603 – which marked the end of the Tudor period – the palace buildings were virtually uninhabitable.

110. Henry Wriothesley, 3rd Earl of Southampton, who was imprisoned in the Tower for his involvement in the Essex rebellion of 1601. He is shown here, with his beloved cat, in his comfortable apartment in the Tower's royal lodgings.

The Tudors and the Tower

In Focus
Tudor Prisoners of the Tower

Even though it was originally built as a fortress and symbol of royal power, the Tower of London is best known today as a place of imprisonment, torture and execution. Between 1100 and 1952 (when the notorious Kray twins were kept there), some 8000 people were incarcerated within its walls for crimes ranging from conspiracy and treason to murder, debt and sorcery. Some were held for days; others for many years. By no means all were locked away in cold, dark, damp rooms. Many lived in luxurious style, surrounded by comfortable furnishings, well-stocked larders, servants and loved ones.

The Tudor period witnessed more victims of royal wrath than any other. Many of those who found themselves in the Tower were subject to new and terrifying methods of forcing confessions. Although the number of recorded cases of torture is relatively small, the threat of it was often enough to make the prisoners give their interrogators all the information they required. It was common practice for stubborn inmates to be shown the instruments of torture. John Gerard, a Jesuit priest imprisoned in the Tower during Elizabeth I's reign, described his terrifying ordeal: 'We went to the torture room in a kind of solemn procession, the attendants walking ahead with lighted candles. The chamber was underground and dark, particularly near the entrance. It was a vast place and every device and instrument of human torture was there. They pointed out some of them to me and said I would try them all' (fig. 114). The most popular forms of torture included the infamous 'rack', whereby the prisoner's legs and arms would be slowly, agonizingly pulled out of their sockets (fig. 113). Likewise, the Scavenger's Daughter, a set of leg, wrist and neck irons that forced the victim into bone-crushing contortions. Other victims were suspended by the wrists – a simple but excruciating torture.

None of these torments awaited the most famous of the Tower prisoners during the Tudor era, for by the time that she entered the fortress, her 'guilt' had already been sufficiently proved. Henry VIII had been so besotted with Anne Boleyn that he had overturned the entire

111. Prisoners' inscriptions carved into the walls of the Beauchamp Tower. Most were carved between 1532 and 1672.

112. Sir Philip Howard, Earl of Arundel, by Henry Barraud. The Earl is depicted in the Beauchamp Tower, where he was held captive for ten years and died a prisoner in 1595. He carved his name into the walls of his cell – one of numerous prisoners to do so. Their 'graffiti' can still be clearly seen today.

religious and political establishment of England so that he could divorce Katherine of Aragon and take her as his bride. But almost as soon as he had married Anne, his ardour had rapidly cooled. The fact that she bore him only another 'useless' daughter (the future Elizabeth I), rather than the son he so craved, sealed her doom.

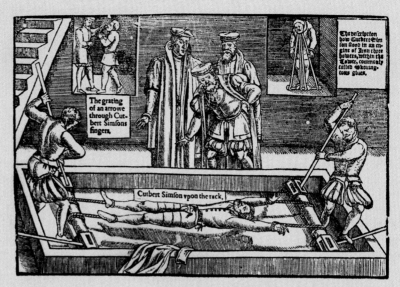

High-handed and 'unqueenly', Anne soon made dangerous enemies at court. Among them was the King's chief minister, Thomas Cromwell, who was almost certainly responsible for her downfall. He drew inspiration from the Queen's flirtatious manner with her coterie of male favourites, and convinced the King that she was conducting adulterous affairs with five of them – her own brother included. Cromwell had them all rounded up, and the Queen herself was arrested on 2 May 1536. She was taken by barge to the Tower, stoutly protesting her innocence all the way, and incarcerated in the same apartments that had been refurbished for her coronation (fig. 115).

Ever resourceful, Anne wrote at once to her husband 'from my doleful prison in the Tower', pleading for justice. But Henry remained unmoved. On 12 May, Mark Smeaton, Sir Henry Norris, Sir Francis Weston and William Brereton were taken from the Tower to Westminster, where they were found guilty of treason and condemned to be beheaded on Tower Hill.

Three days later, Anne herself was tried, along with her brother, George. Rather than being taken to Westminster, they faced their accusers at the Tower, in the Great Hall of the royal palace. The beleaguered Queen calmly and eloquently defended herself against the trumped-up charges, but in vain. The King was so confident of the verdict that he had already ordered an expert swordsman from Calais to carry out the sentence.

Anne watched as her five alleged lovers were led to their deaths on Tower Hill on 17 May. She was told to prepare for her own death the following day. Although she remained composed, when her execution was delayed for a further day, she became almost hysterical. The Constable of the Tower, Sir William Kingston, looked on aghast as she put her hands around her neck and pronounced that the executioner should have no trouble because 'I have a little neck', then 'laughed heartily'.

113. *(top) One of the most horrific forms of torture was the rack, by which the victim's arms and legs would be wrenched from their sockets. This illustration, taken from John Foxe's* Acts and Monuments, *shows the Protestant deacon Cuthbert Simpson being racked by the Catholic Queen Mary's interrogators. The inset pictures show the other torments that he suffered.*

114. *Father John Gerard, a Jesuit priest, was imprisoned in the Tower during the reign of the Protestant Queen Elizabeth I. He was tortured twice (he is shown here suspended by manacles in the White Tower), but later escaped from the Tower. He used orange juice as invisible ink to send messages to his friends.*

115. *(below)* Anne Boleyn in the Tower of London, shortly after her Arrest by Edouard Cibot, 1835. Henry VIII's second wife was tried for treason in the Great Hall of the Tower, which had been renovated for her coronation three years earlier. She was executed at the Tower on 19 May 1536.

116. *Thomas Cromwell, chief minister to Henry VIII, who fell foul of the King after arranging his ill-fated marriage to Anne of Cleves. He was imprisoned in the Tower in June 1540 and executed on Tower Hill the following month.*

EARL OF ESSEX.

Finally, on the morning of 19 May 1536, Anne was led from her apartments to the scaffold. After a dignified speech, she knelt in the straw and closed her eyes to pray. With a clean strike, the Calais executioner severed her head from her body. The 1000-strong crowd looked on aghast as the fallen Queen's eyes and lips continued to move, as if in silent prayer, when the head was held aloft.

When the spectators had finally dispersed, Anne's weeping ladies sought in vain for a coffin in which to lay their mistress's body. All they could find was an old arrow chest, and it was in this that Henry's second queen was laid to rest in the Chapel of St Peter ad Vincula.

Anne's nemesis, Thomas Cromwell, had been among the onlookers at this macabre spectacle (fig. 116). His triumph would be short-lived. Four years later, he was summarily arrested on charges of treason by the captain of the royal guard and conveyed by barge to the Tower. He may have been housed in the same lodgings in which Anne had been kept before her execution.

Cromwell wrote to beg the King for his life, ending with a desperate plea for 'mercye mercye mercye'. Henry remained unmoved, and Cromwell went to the block on 28 July 1540. The bungling executioner took three blows to sever his head, which was then set on a spike on London Bridge, as so many had been before. In an act of extreme callousness, later that day Henry married his fifth wife, Catherine Howard, who would herself be executed at the Tower a mere eighteen months later. But he soon came to regret his minister's demise. Within a few short months, according to one ambassador, he was lamenting the loss of 'the most faithful servant he had ever had'.

Henry VIII had demonstrated that he was no respecter of rank when it came to putting his perceived enemies to death. But even he might have been shocked at the other high-profile prisoner to fall victim to the Tudor regime. In March 1554 his own daughter Elizabeth followed the horribly familiar journey by barge from Westminster to the Tower. On the accession of her half-sister, Mary I, the previous year, Elizabeth

had been high in favour and had taken pride of place in the new Queen's triumphant procession through London. But Mary had soon come to resent her beautiful, charismatic sibling, who steadfastly resisted her entreaties to conform to the traditional Catholic faith. Resentment soon turned to suspicion. Within a few short months of Mary's accession, Thomas Wyatt led a revolt to place Elizabeth on the throne (fig. 117). The Tower was prepared to defend the capital against the rebels, but the new defences ordered by Thomas Cromwell in the early 1530s proved ineffective. An eyewitness noted that as soon as the rebels were within view, 'ther was shot off out of the White Tower a vi or viii shot, but myssed them, sometymes shoting over and sometimes shoting short'.

Even though Elizabeth was almost certainly innocent of any involvement in the plot, Mary was taking no chances: she had her sister brought to the Tower. It was a cold, wet March day when Elizabeth arrived at the fortress. As she slowly mounted the steps next to Traitors' Gate, she suddenly stopped and exclaimed: 'Oh Lord! I never thought to have come in here as a prisoner; and I pray you all, good friends and fellows, bear me witness, that I come in no traitor, but as true woman to the queen's majesty as any is now living.' She was eventually persuaded to move on into the Tower, and was taken to the same royal lodgings where her mother had been held prisoner prior to her execution (fig. 118). She is reputed to have scratched the following rhyme on her window with a diamond ring: 'Much suspected by me – nothing proved can be.'

Among Elizabeth's fellow prisoners was her future favourite, Robert Dudley, who was incarcerated with four of his brothers after their father, the Duke of Northumberland, tried to oust Mary from power. The rebel Wyatt was also imprisoned at the Tower at the same time as Elizabeth, but only until 11 April 1554, when he was led up to Tower Hill for his execution.

Elizabeth was finally allowed to leave the Tower on 19 May – eighteen years to the day since her mother had been executed within the fortress. The irony cannot have been lost on her.

117. (above) Sir Thomas Wyatt, who led a rebellion against 'Bloody' Mary Tudor in 1554, aimed at putting her half-sister, Elizabeth, on the throne.

118. Princess Elizabeth in the Tower by Emanuel Gottlieb Leutze, 1860. Elizabeth was imprisoned in the fortress in 1554 on suspicion of involvement in the Wyatt rebellion. On arriving at Traitors' Gate, the Princess cried: 'Oh Lord! I never thought to have come in here as a prisoner.'

Gunpowder, Treason and Plot

The death of Elizabeth I on 24 March 1603 ushered in not just a new ruler but a new dynasty. James VI of Scotland became James I (1603–25) of a united, Stuart kingdom. On the very day of his arrival in London, the King paid a visit to the Tower and stayed there for several nights. After witnessing the impressive sight of the cannon on the roof of the White Tower being fired, he was shown, according to a contemporary account, the 'Armorie, the Wardrobe, the rich Artillerie and the Church'. The following day, he inspected the 'Ordinance-house and after the Mynt-house, and last of all the Lyons'.

The subsequent repairs to the royal lodgings in preparation for James's coronation suggest that by that time they had become somewhat dilapidated. The roof had collapsed and a temporary covering had to be hastily erected so that the occupants were not exposed to the elements. There was so little suitable accommodation for the King's ministers that some high-profile prisoners had to be moved to make room for them.

The prisoners included Sir Walter Ralegh, whom James had imprisoned on suspicion of conspiracy just a few weeks after his accession (fig. 121). Ralegh was kept in two rooms on the upper floor

119. (previous pages) Soldiers parading outside the Tower in the seventeenth century; see fig. 125.

120. Sir Walter Ralegh enjoyed comfortable lodgings in the Bloody Tower. The lower chamber shown here contains a good fireplace, a large window, which once had window seats, and a floor of richly decorated tiles.

121. *Sir Walter Ralegh. A great favourite of Elizabeth I, Ralegh was despised by her successor, James I, who had him imprisoned in the Tower shortly after his accession in 1603. Ralegh was eventually executed in 1618.*

Gunpowder, Treason and Plot

122. The Gunpowder Plot conspirators, 1605. Led by Robert Catesby, the group of Catholic gentlemen hatched a plan to blow up the House of Lords during the State Opening of Parliament on 5 November 1605. After their plot was discovered, they were rounded up and sent to the Tower.

of the Bloody Tower, and his faithful wife, Bess, often stayed with him (fig. 120). Their son Carew was conceived in the fortress and born in 1605 in a house on Tower Hill that Bess had rented. Ralegh also passed the time by writing his *History of the World*, an epic work and certainly the longest of the Tower's literary outputs. He became something of a tourist attraction during his prolonged spell in the Tower. The King's own son and heir, Prince Henry, went to visit him. He was so dazzled by Ralegh's famous charm that he declared: 'Only my father would cage such a bird.' Ralegh was finally released in 1616 so that he could conduct an expedition to Venezuela to find the fabled 'El Dorado' or City of Gold, but on his ignominious return James had him thrown back into the Tower. This time there was no reprieve: Ralegh was executed at Westminster on 29 October 1618. His grief-stricken widow, Bess, kept his severed, embalmed head with her for the rest of her days.

The Tower housed another famous prisoner during the reign of James I. When it became clear that the new King had no intention of following Elizabeth I's policy of religious toleration, a group of conspirators led by Robert Catesby hatched a plan to blow up the House of Lords during the State Opening of Parliament on 5 November 1605. It was only thanks to an anonymous letter to the authorities, received in late October, that the King and his Protestant regime were not wiped out. The House of Lords was searched at around midnight on 4 November, just hours before the plot was due to be executed, and Guy Fawkes was discovered with thirty-six barrels of gunpowder – more than enough to reduce the entire building to rubble. Fawkes was

The Story of The Tower of London

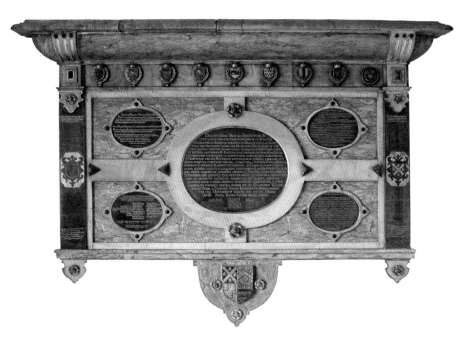

123. (left) A marble
monument to the
Gunpowder Plot,
erected at the Tower
by the Lieutenant,
Sir William Waad, in
1608. The conspirators
were interrogated (and
tortured) in the Queen's
House before suffering
traitors' deaths
at Westminster.

124. Sir Thomas Overbury
by Silvester Harding,
after Marcus Gheeraerts
the Younger. Overbury
suffered a prolonged and
agonizing death by poison
while a prisoner in the
Bloody Tower. It was one
of the most notorious and
controversial scandals in
the Tower's history.

taken straight to the Tower, and was soon joined by his fellow plotters
(fig. 122). They were interrogated in the Queen's House, where there
is an important monument commemorating the event today (fig. 123).
Fawkes eventually confessed after suffering the agony of the rack. The
shaky signature on his confession suggests that he was barely able to
hold a pen. He and his fellow conspirators met grisly traitors' deaths at
Westminster in January 1606. It is said that the gunpowder with which
they had planned to obliterate James's regime was taken to the Tower
for safe keeping.

As his reign progressed, James became ever more unpopular. He
had few personal graces to recommend him, and his homosexual
liaisons with a succession of male courtiers excited gossip and derision
in equal measure. One of James's closest favourites was a handsome
fellow Scot named Robert Carr. Politically inept, Carr relied heavily on
his friend and admirer Sir Thomas Overbury, who conducted a great
deal of business for him (fig. 124). He even wrote love letters on Carr's
behalf to Frances Howard, Countess of Essex, a beautiful but ruthless
courtier. But when it became clear that Carr intended to marry Frances,
Overbury feared that his own hold over him would be destroyed, so
he set about trying to disrupt the match. Determined to get rid of this
irksome opponent, the Countess's ambitious family persuaded the King
to arrest Overbury on trumped-up charges, and he was taken to the
Tower. He would never leave it.

Lodged in the ground floor of the Bloody Tower, beneath the rooms
of Sir Walter Ralegh, Overbury became the victim of a notorious

murder plot. Working with accomplices in the Tower, the Howards arranged for Overbury to be slowly, agonizingly poisoned. Draughts of arsenic and mercury were mixed into his food, which caused frequent bouts of vomiting and made the unfortunate prisoner's skin break out in painful boils and blisters. But Overbury was made of stronger stuff than they anticipated, and survived this torment for five long months before finally succumbing to a fatal dose of mercury on 15 September 1613. His body was hastily buried at St Peter ad Vincula. It was not until two years later that the plot was uncovered, and Carr and his now wife, Frances, were thrown into the Tower – in the very same cell where Overbury had suffered so cruelly. Their accomplices were executed, but the Carrs were eventually pardoned in 1622.

Like his Tudor predecessors, James had come to view the Tower more as a prison than a residence. He also showed little inclination to make the necessary repairs to its fortifications. The problem of private houses and workshops encroaching on the moat and up against the western entrance, thereby weakening the security of the fortress, had been highlighted by a report of 1600. By 1623, when another survey was taken, as many as 220 houses, sheds, timber yards and the like had sprung up along the moat. James chose not to redress the situation, and neither did he heed the recommendations for repairs to the moat.

James's son Charles I (1625–49) was not able to ignore such concerns, however. Within ten years of his accession, he had alienated swathes of his subjects through his arrogance and flagrant disregard of Parliament. Realizing that the Tower was, as he put it, a 'bridle upon the city', Charles resolved to bolster its supplies and defences. In 1636 part of the White Tower was converted into a powder store and a large doorway was punched through the external wall to allow supplies to be hauled in from outside (fig. 143). During the next two years, the external appearance of the White Tower was significantly altered, with the replacement of much of its cut-stone work and window surrounds with

125. Soldiers parading outside the Tower in the seventeenth century. The military role of the fortress was greatly enhanced during this period, owing to the onset of the Civil War and later the need of the restored King, Charles II, to secure his throne.

The Story of The Tower of London

Portland stone, probably by the celebrated architect Inigo Jones. In 1639 the whole of the exterior was whitewashed – perhaps for the last time in its history.

By 1640 the country was on the brink of civil war. In response, Charles ordered new gun platforms to be built at the Tower, swelled the arsenal of weaponry and drafted in trained bands of militia (fig. 125). But it was all in vain. The King was obliged to flee London after his ill-advised attempt to arrest five members of the House of Commons in January 1642, and the Tower was taken by Parliamentarian forces without a single shot being fired.

By the time that war broke out in September 1642, the Tower was firmly in the hands of Oliver Cromwell and his men, giving them such a substantial advantage over the King that it would help to decide the outcome of the Civil War (fig. 127). During the years that followed, the fortress became so crammed with Royalist prisoners that it was estimated that one third of the entire House of Lords had been incarcerated there. Cromwell's triumph was sealed on 30 January 1649, when King Charles was executed outside the Banqueting House, Whitehall.

Shortly afterwards, the contents of the Royal Wardrobe were sold off (fig. 126). An inventory that was taken at the time reveals how extensive – and valuable – these items had become. They included hangings priced at £18,000, and £3000 worth of other textiles and furnishings. The sale of its contents signalled the end of the Tower Wardrobe, and the following year the empty buildings were turned into storage for gunpowder.

126. (left) An entry in an inventory of the contents of the Tower Wardrobe, taken after Henry VIII's death in 1547. Most of the treasures, including the crimson chair 'fringed with Venice gold' (listed here), were destroyed or dispersed in 1649 by the new republican regime.

127. Before Civil War broke out, Charles I attempted to secure the Tower against the Parliamentarians, but it was soon under the control of Oliver Cromwell (pictured here) and his men.

The Jewel in the Crown

128. (previous pages) The Great Fire of London, 1666, with the Tower shown on the right; see fig. 135.

129. Sir John Robinson, Lord Mayor, by John Michael Wright, 1662. At the Restoration, Robinson was in command of the Tower, performing the duties of both Constable and Lieutenant. The White Tower is depicted in the background of this portrait.

The restoration of the monarchy with Charles II (1660–85) heralded a new era in the Tower's history. The austerity of the post–Civil War years was at an end, and the ostentation, pomp and pageantry of royal authority was back in dazzling style (fig. 129). As an age-old symbol of royal power, the Tower was about to enter the spotlight once more.

Soon after his accession, Charles established what would become known as the Line of Kings. Originally displayed in the House of Ordnance (see page 128), this was a series of life-size figures representing the monarchs of England, each one of whom was mounted on a carved wooden horse and – with the exception of Elizabeth I – shown in the splendour of his full armour. The earliest monarch on display was William the Conqueror, and Charles II's own effigy was added in 1685. The aim of the display was to demonstrate the unbroken line of kingship – the unfortunate blip of the Commonwealth being well and truly forgotten (fig. 131). The line was added to over the centuries that followed, and has now been restored and dramatically redisplayed in the White Tower.

The Story of The Tower of London

130. *A portrait of Charles I by Daniel Mytens, 1631, showing the State Crown made for Henry VII or Henry VIII and kept at the Tower Jewel House until its destruction by Oliver Cromwell's men in 1649.*

131. *The Line of Kings in 1809, when housed in the New Armouries building. This series of life-size figures represented the monarchs of England, each one mounted on a carved wooden horse. The line has recently been redisplayed in the White Tower.*

Determined to re-establish royal ceremonies, Charles observed the centuries-old tradition of riding out from the Tower to his coronation. It is a sign of how dilapidated the royal quarters had become, however, that he was unable to spend the night there. Now that the Tower had fallen out of use as a royal residence, the tradition would die with Charles. Over the two centuries that followed, the royal apartments would be systematically demolished, and the thirteenth-century St Thomas's and Wakefield towers are now the only survivals.

Before Charles could be crowned, he was obliged to commission a new set of coronation regalia (fig. 132). In 1649 his father's nemesis, Oliver Cromwell, had ordered all of the royal jewels and plate to be brought to the Tower of London and either destroyed or sold. The crowns – the most potent symbols of royal power – were 'totally broken and defaced', and the metal was sent to the Mint to be made into coinage (fig. 130).

The collection of royal jewels, which was started by Henry III in the thirteenth century, had been housed at the Tower for safe keeping ever since the reign of his son and successor, Edward I. The Crown Jewels, as they became known, had experienced mixed fortunes ever since. A number of cash-strapped monarchs, such as Edward III and

The Story of The Tower of London

Richard II, had pawned them abroad, but the Tudors, realizing their symbolic importance, had built up the collection into a treasury of great value. They had also commissioned a highly secure 'Jewel House', adjacent to the White Tower, complete with bars at the windows and iron chests to store the most precious items.

James I had taken a keen interest in the dazzling collection that he had inherited from his Tudor predecessors. On his accession, he had signed an inventory that had been prepared of the jewels. It provides a glimpse into the richness of this eclectic collection, which included

132. To mark the restoration of the monarchy in 1660, Charles II commissioned a lavish new collection of Crown Jewels to replace those melted down by Oliver Cromwell in 1649. The orb and sceptre he holds here have been used at every coronation since.

133. The twelfth-century 'Coronation Spoon', one of only a handful of items to escape the destruction of the regalia in 1649. It was kept safe by a Royalist supporter and returned to Charles II in 1660.

134. (opposite) The Imperial State Crown, made for the coronation of George VI in 1937 and altered for his daughter, Queen Elizabeth II, in 1953. The stone in the centre is the Black Prince's Ruby.

fifteen gold collars studded with diamonds and other precious stones, a coronet and circlet set with priceless jewels, and a 'long pece of unicorn horn' and other exotica that Elizabeth I's adventurers had brought back from their travels. The new King had further enhanced this already impressive collection with some choice items, such as a richly jewelled coronet made for his Queen, Anne of Denmark.

On the eve of the destruction of the collection by Oliver Cromwell, another inventory of the Crown Jewels had been drawn up. It included an imperial crown of 'massy gold', weighing a hefty 3.3 kilograms (7 lb 6 oz) and worth £1110, making it by far the most valuable item in the collection. There were also numerous diamonds, rubies, sapphires and other precious stones, along with the sceptre and orb used in coronation ceremonies. Among the oldest items to be consigned to the melting pot were two ancient Saxon crowns, reputedly worn by King Alfred the Great and Queen Edith, wife of Edward the Confessor.

The only items that had been saved were a coronation anointing spoon (fig. 133), some ceremonial swords, a silver salt cellar once belonging to Elizabeth I, and the Black Prince's Ruby. The latter (which was technically a spinel, not a ruby proper) was by far the most impressive – and valuable. About the size of a small chicken's egg, this blood-red stone had, according to legend, been given to Edward III's eldest son, Edward, the Black Prince, by Pedro the Cruel, King of Castile and Leon, to thank him for helping to restore him to power in 1367. The jewel had stayed in the royal family and was set into the crown worn by Henry V at Agincourt in 1415. Perhaps in the hope that it would bring him the same luck, Richard III reputedly wore it in his crown at the Battle of Bosworth in 1485. Legend has it that the crown fell from the ill-fated King's head as he was overcome by Henry VII's forces and was later found under a hawthorn bush – the ruby still intact.

The stone continued to adorn the crowns of the kings and queens of England during the Tudor and Stuart dynasties, and it was saved from destruction by Oliver Cromwell only thanks to a secret Royalist sympathizer, who bought it for the paltry sum of £4 before the crown was sent to the furnace. He carefully preserved it until Charles II's restoration in 1660, when it was restored to its place at the front of the King's new State Crown (fig. 134).

Charles's court jeweller, Sir Robert Vyner, was entrusted with the challenging but prestigious task of making a suite of new jewels to accompany the crown. In order to emphasize the continuity of the

135. The Great Fire of London, 1666. The Tower, shown on the right, narrowly escaped damage, largely thanks to the swift removal of the huge quantities of gunpowder that were stored in the White Tower.

136. (opposite) Queen Elizabeth II at her coronation in 1953, wearing her father George VI's Imperial State Crown. She is holding the orb and sceptre made for Charles II in 1660.

monarchy, Vyner was instructed to make the new jewels as much like the lost originals as possible. Fortunately, he was assisted by detailed records preserved at the Tower. The result was the dazzling array of regalia that has been used by the royal family ever since (fig. 136).

The new Crown Jewels were housed in the ground floor of the Martin Tower, with the Keeper's apartments above. Arrangements were made for members of the public to view them on display, and from that time forward, they became the most visited attraction within the Tower of London (fig. 139).

However, the collection came under threat soon after its inception. In the early hours of 2 September 1666, the diarist Samuel Pepys hastened to the Tower from his home in nearby Seething Lane. A fire had broken out in a baker's shop on Pudding Lane, a short walk from the Tower. Pepys climbed to a high window in the White Tower so that he could get a sufficiently good vantage point to assess the damage. To his dismay, he saw that the inferno had spread at a terrifying rate and looked set to consume the entire city (fig. 135). He raced from the Tower and hired a boat to Whitehall Palace so that he might tell King Charles the dreadful news.

The Story of The Tower of London

The Jewel in the Crown

Meanwhile, at the Tower there was great consternation because of the vast quantity of gunpowder that was stored in the White Tower arsenal. A desperate effort was launched to remove it. Royal Navy seamen worked with a team of civilians to carry barrels laden with gunpowder out of the fortress and into waiting ships bound for Woolwich and Greenwich. This was an extremely hazardous task: the sky was filled with sparks from the flames, any one of which could have detonated a huge blast. Pepys's friend and fellow diarist John Evelyn speculated what would have happened if the fire had reached the gunpowder store before it was conveyed to safety. The enormous explosion 'would undoubtedly have not only beaten down and destroyed all the [London] Bridge, but sunk and torn all the vessels in the river and rendered the demolition beyond all expression for several miles even about the country at many miles distance'. Thankfully, and somewhat against the odds, every last barrel was removed from the Tower. But the fortress would still have been prey to the rapidly intensifying fire had it not been for a decision by the authorities to stop the progress of the flames by blowing up buildings at key strategic positions near by.

The Tower – and its precious contents – had survived the Great Fire of London. But the 220 houses and warehouses along the moat that had posed a security threat for many years had been purposely destroyed within hours in order to prevent the flames sweeping across to the fortress. The whole question of the Tower's security was considered again in the wake of the catastrophe, and in November 1666 the Ordnance Chief Engineer, Sir Bernard de Gomme, was engaged in 'makeinge a draught of [the] Tower and designe of fortifienge the same'. Although his ambitious scheme never reached fruition, certain elements of it were taken forward. Most importantly, improvements to the moat were finally carried out, and a massive brick revetment was built on the western and northern banks between 1670 and 1672. The retaining wall was later continued down the east side of the moat, and the entire length of it fenced off with a wooden 'Raile ... to prevent peoples falling in'. Meanwhile, the old Bulwark, built by Edward IV to reinforce the western entrance, was demolished and replaced in 1670 by a new wall and gate to the north of the Lion Tower.

137. An eighteenth-century engraving of Colonel Blood's attempt to steal the Crown Jewels in 1671. Blood is the central figure dressed as a clergyman; he is holding the bag into which his accomplice is putting the sceptre.

The Story of The Tower of London

The new fortifications did little to deter one infamous intruder, however. In 1671 'Colonel' Thomas Blood, a mercenary who had fought in the Civil War, staged an audacious attempt to steal the star items of the Crown Jewels. Posing as a clergyman, he befriended Talbot Edwards, the elderly Jewel House Keeper, and paid several visits to the Jewel House that spring. As soon as Blood had amassed enough information about the security arrangements, he put his daring plan into action.

On the morning of 9 May 1671, Blood visited the Martin Tower once more, but this time accompanied by his son Thomas, his friend Robert Perot, and a notorious thug named Richard Halliwell. The unsuspecting Edwards was only too happy to show Blood and his friends the jewels and led the way downstairs to the storeroom. But while Halliwell stood guard outside the door, Blood and his gang bound the elderly Keeper's hands and rammed a piece of wood in his mouth. Edwards struggled so much that he was stabbed and beaten about the head. In haste, Blood flattened the State Crown with a mallet and instructed his son to saw the sceptre in half, while Perot stuffed the orb down his breeches (fig. 137). But just as they were about to make their escape, Edwards's son returned unexpectedly from the army after several years abroad. He raised the alarm and Blood's gang made a run for it, but were apprehended while they were still within the walls of the fortress.

138. The Arrival of Venetian Ambassadors at the Tower Stairs, May 1707 *by the Italian artist Luca Carlevaris. Although the Tower had ceased to be used as a royal residence, it retained its symbolic significance.*

Blood and his associates were imprisoned in the vaults beneath the White Tower. But the 'Colonel' remained remarkably calm during his interrogation. He demanded an audience with the King, which was granted. Not long after, although Blood deserved a traitor's death, Charles not only pardoned him, but also granted him lands in his native Ireland and a pension of £500 a year. This prompted speculation as to the true nature of the supposed crime. Had Blood simply talked his way out of trouble, or had he been working as a double agent all along?

Security measures were evidently tightened after this alarming episode. A visitor to the Tower in 1710 described how, after entering 'a gloomy and cramped den', a strong door was bolted from within and outside. Visitors were then obliged to sit on wooden benches and view the jewels through 'a trellis work of strong iron'. This restrictive experience did not obscure the beauty of the treasures, however, for the same contemporary observer noted that the display 'looks very well and sparkles charmingly because they have lights there on account of the gloom'. Later visitors were less complimentary. In 1821 Christian Goede published a damning account in *A Foreigner's Opinion of England*, describing how a 'ghastly' old woman 'takes some sceptres and crowns out of a couple of old boxes, shows them to him through an iron grate, and chants with a shrill voice the list and story of these wonderful curiosities, with which the whole farce is most stupidly concluded'.

In 1840 the decision was finally taken to build a more commodious and secure Jewel House. This Gothic-style building was attached to the south side of the Martin Tower and opened to the public two years later (fig. 140). Although it had been specifically designed to house the jewels, it was a grave disappointment to visitors, who complained about the damp and poor lighting. Neither were the security measures sufficient. In 1866 the regalia were moved to the Wakefield Tower, where they remained until 1967, when the sheer volume of visitors prompted the building of a new Jewel House underneath the Waterloo Barracks (fig. 141). They have been housed in this building ever since.

139. An engraving of c. 1820 showing the Crown Jewels on display in the Martin Tower. A Yeoman Warder tells the visitors about the regalia, which include the State Crown under the glass dome on the left.

140. (above) The short-lived Jewel House of 1842. Visitors soon complained about the poor lighting and damp, and the collection was subsequently moved to the Wakefield Tower, where it remained until 1967.

141. A photograph of c. 1905 showing the Crown Jewels on display in the Wakefield Tower. In 1967 the collection was moved from there to its current home in the Waterloo Barracks.

The Jewel in the Crown

In Focus
The Royal Arsenal and Garrison

Charles II's reign might have witnessed the creation of a dazzling new set of Crown Jewels, but the arsenal of weapons at the Tower, which had been the largest in the country since the late Middle Ages, began to decline (fig. 142).

The Office of Ordnance (later known as the Board of Ordnance) and the Office of Armoury had been the most influential occupants of the fortress since the fifteenth century. Their importance was owing to the absence of a standing army until 1661, which made it crucial that weapons could be quickly and efficiently supplied to troops that were raised for particular needs. The main stores managed by the two offices comprised armour, edged weapons, handguns, ordnance (heavier weapons and cannon) and gunpowder.

By the end of the fifteenth century, the main 'House of Ordnance' stood across the north side of the Inner Ward, facing the White Tower. Additional storage space was provided at the top of the White Tower itself. In 1545 Henry VIII granted funds to 'erect and newe buylde one howse wherein all the Kinges Ordinance and Municions maye be kepte'. This resulted in a vast new building on the same site – the largest of any within the Tower – which spread all the way along the inner north wall of the Tower, from the Devereux Tower in the west to the Martin Tower in the east. Referred to as the 'Ordinnannce Howse' in an order dated 1552, it was fully equipped to accommodate the ever-expanding array of weapons in the royal arsenal.

During the remainder of the Tudor period, the Ordnance gradually encroached on more of the existing areas within the fortress, including the royal lodgings and White Tower – the latter being the principal

142. The Tower from the Thames, c. 1660. The small warship in the foreground is a reminder of the castle's importance as a repository of weaponry and other military supplies, although by this time it had lost its position as the country's greatest arsenal.

The Story of The Tower of London

repository for the huge quantity of gunpowder that was stored in the fortress.

By the advent of the English Civil War in 1642, growing concern about the security of the Tower and its weaponry prompted the drafting in of local militia to hold the fortress on the King's behalf. Until that time, there had been only a small guard of Yeoman Warders (royal bodyguards), along with some gunners and the occasional attendance of men from Tower Hamlets who 'owe thier service to the Towre ... for the defence of the same'. Although Charles I's garrison failed to secure the fortress for the Royalists, the attempt inspired his adversary, Oliver Cromwell, to establish a permanent garrison at the Tower.

After the restoration of the monarchy in 1660, the Tower lost its position as the greatest arsenal in the country. The defence of Britain's overseas empire required larger facilities than the fortress could provide, so new weaponry repositories were developed at such sites as Woolwich, Chatham, Portsmouth and Plymouth. Nevertheless, the Tower continued to function as the main administrative base for supplies, and by 1664 a new storehouse was completed on the eastern side, close to the Wardrobe Tower. It has been known as the 'New Armouries' ever since.

As well as continuing its practical role as a base for munitions, the Tower also increasingly acted as a showcase for some of the more interesting and spectacular pieces of weaponry. Henry VIII had been particularly fond of showing off his impressive array of arms, and a visitor to the Tower during the reign of his daughter Elizabeth I was amazed by the gilt suit of armour and several historic cannon that he was shown (fig. 144). Jacob Rathgeb, secretary to Frederick, Duke of Württemberg, was less impressed. He visited the Tower Armoury in 1592 and complained that the items on display were 'full of dust and stand about in the greatest confusion and disorder'.

It was not until the second half of the seventeenth century that four new displays of weaponry were created specifically for public view: the Line of Kings (see page 116; figs. 131 and 145); the Small Armoury (fig. 146), a magnificent collection of thousands of small arms displayed in the Grand Storehouse (page 131); the Artillery Room, displaying large cannon; and the Spanish Armoury. The Spanish Armoury was a collection of fearsome-looking weapons and a few instruments of torture, allegedly

143. A medal struck during the Restoration to commemorate the sufferings of the Royalists during the Interregnum. The north elevation of the White Tower is depicted, and shows the various doorways and hatches cut through it to facilitate the movement of stores in and out of the building.

144. The 'mighty burdensome' armour of Henry VIII, which has been on display to Tower visitors since 1599. The suit was commissioned in 1540 for one of the last tournaments that Henry was known to have organized. The great size of the armour indicates how much weight the King had put on in his later years.

145. (right) A view of the White Tower in the 1870s. The low building to the left is the Horse Armoury, built in 1825 to house the Line of Kings.

146. The Small Armoury on the first floor of the Grand Storehouse in 1822. The columns, pilasters and other features are all festooned with weapons, making it an impressive sight for visitors.

taken from the Armada of 1588. Installed in Henry VIII's old ordnance house to the north of the White Tower until its demolition in 1688, the Spanish Armoury was then redisplayed in a storehouse erected immediately north of the Wakefield Tower in 1670–71. The outbreak of war with Spain in 1779 prompted the installation of an equestrian figure of Elizabeth I addressing the English forces at Tilbury. On the accession of Queen Victoria in 1837, the display (now called Queen Elizabeth's Armoury) was moved to the crypt of the White Tower chapel.

As part of his programme of improvements at the Tower, Charles II had turned his attention to the garrison's accommodation. Between 1669 and 1670 the first purpose-built soldiers' lodgings were constructed against the curtain wall between the Salt and Broad Arrow towers. The 'Irish Barracks', as it became known, was a simple timber-framed building with a weather-boarded exterior.

Despite these improvements, however, the condition of the Tower's garrison and defences was still considered inadequate, and a series of further recommendations was made in 1682. These won Charles II's approval, and during the next six years virtually all thirty-two recommendations were acted upon, which constituted a substantial programme of work (fig. 148). This included the building of timber gun platforms against the outer curtain wall, and the raising of Legge's Mount by 5.8 metres (19 ft) in order to accommodate two tiers of guns. Meanwhile, various coach houses and stables were converted into accommodation for soldiers and gunners, and a new barrack block was built in the Mint. The old Main Guard, located to the south-east of the Beauchamp Tower, was demolished and a new one constructed near the north-west corner of the White Tower.

Another report, in 1687, by the Master-General of the Ordnance, George Legge, prompted a more ambitious building project. He warned of the 'crazy condition' of the sprawling sixteenth-century storehouses to the north of the White Tower. The following year, work began on the Grand Storehouse, which, when completed in 1692, was the largest single ordnance store in the world (figs. 147 and 149).

147. (above) The Grand Storehouse, completed in 1692. This impressive building, measuring 110 metres (360 ft) long and 18 metres (60 ft) wide, replaced the Ordnance storehouse built by Henry VIII.

148. A view of the Tower from the west, by Johann Spilberg II, c. 1691. The rows of newly installed cannon can be seen along the ramparts. These had been commissioned as a result of a damning report on the Tower's garrison and defences drawn up in 1682.

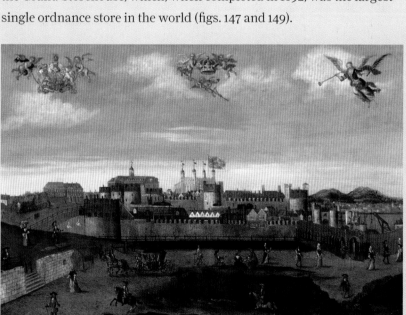

In Focus: The Royal Arsenal and Garrison

Meanwhile, attention was paid to the military personnel of the Tower, as well as the buildings. During the Lieutenantship of Sir John Robinson (1660–79; see fig. 129), a set of strict regulations was issued, dictating that no officer or soldier should 'blaspheme Gods Holy Name by Oaths, Executions, or Scandalous actions' or 'ease themselves in any place than that appointed for that purpose'. New fines were introduced for all offences, which included enduring three days 'in the hole' for the improper firing of muskets within the confines of the Tower.

149. (above) On the night of 30 October 1841, a devastating fire ripped through the Grand Storehouse. The huge crowds that gathered to watch can be seen at the bottom of the painting. The new Mint is on the left, lit up by the flames.

150. The late eighteenth-century Ordnance Offices in 1883. The upper floors had been added during the Crimean War (1853–56).

The newly disciplined garrison helped to keep the peace in the surrounding area, as well as protecting the Tower. In the absence of any true police force, this was an important task, and the district over which it had control gradually spread. Thus, in 1693 a regiment was sent to break up a riot in Southwark, while in 1697 troops were dispatched to Westminster to help suppress another uprising.

The Story of The Tower of London

During the remainder of the seventeenth and into the eighteenth century there followed a rapid expansion of accommodation for the storage and administration of the weaponry. New offices were constructed for the Ordnance immediately north of the Lanthorn Tower, incorporating part of the medieval Queen's Lodgings. Following a fire in 1774, the offices were rebuilt on the same site in a neoclassical style (fig. 150). At the beginning of George I's reign in 1714, an Ordnance Drawing Room was created. A precursor to the Ordnance Survey, which like many great institutions had its origins in the Tower, this little-known development would make a major contribution to the training of British military surveyors and draughtsmen.

George I (1714–27) and his successor, George II (1727–60), had good reason to bolster the Tower's defences. The Jacobites, supporters of the son and grandson of the ousted King James II (1685–88) – respectively

151. (above) The execution of the Jacobite rebels Lord Balmerino and Earl Kilmarnock on Tower Hill in 1746. They were among the last prisoners to be executed there. Vast crowds would gather to witness these grisly spectacles, and special viewing platforms were erected along the edge of the Tower moat.

152. An illustration from a guide to the Tower of c. 1820, showing three of its most popular attractions: instruments of torture and weaponry, the Line of Kings and the Menagerie.

153. A view of the Tower from the east in 1804. In the foreground are the buildings of the 'Arms manufactory' built in 1803 to cope with the extra demand for weapons during the Napoleonic Wars.

known as the Old and Young Pretenders – aimed to supplant the Hanoverians and restore the Stuarts to the throne (fig. 151). One of the most high-profile Jacobite rebels was the Scottish peer William Maxwell, 5th Earl of Nithsdale, who declared the Old Pretender King James in the Scottish Borders before joining the English Jacobite army in Northumberland. King George I's army quashed the rebel forces at the Battle of Preston in 1715, and Nithsdale was brought south to the Tower along with the other ringleaders.

On hearing of her beloved husband's capture, Lady Nithsdale – herself a fervent Jacobite – hastened to London to plead for his life. But George was not minded to show clemency towards this dangerous rebel peer. Undaunted, she hatched a daring escape plan for her husband, which involved dressing him in women's clothes (including a cloak, which still survives), painting his face with cosmetics and walking past the guards with his head bowed, as if he were in great distress. This part of the plan was carried out with remarkable success, and Lord Nithsdale made it out of the Tower to a waiting coach, which carried him to safety. Meanwhile, in order to delay the discovery, his wife remained in the cell and pretended to conduct a conversation with her husband, imitating his deep masculine voice. Finally, she let herself out, slamming the door behind her and pleading with the guards not to disturb Nithsdale, who was deep in prayer. Once reunited, the couple fled to Rome, where they lived out their days, poor but happy.

The Story of The Tower of London

At least partly in response to the Jacobite threat, the accommodation of the Tower garrison also continued to improve during the eighteenth century, with the construction of a new barracks. By the middle of that century, the Irish Barracks were already beyond repair, so a well-proportioned block was built, comprising three storeys and an attic. The same architect, Dugal Campbell, also designed the Spur Barracks, which provided further accommodation on the site of the old Lion Tower moat, and a new guardhouse was erected just north of the Middle Tower.

It was not until the middle of the following century, though, that adequate accommodation was finally provided in the form of the Waterloo Barracks, which were commissioned by the Constable, the Duke of Wellington (fig. 154). Later named after his most famous victory, this vast new building was erected on the site of the Grand Storehouse (which had been destroyed by a fire in 1841) and could accommodate 1000 men. Separate officers' quarters were built to the north-east of the White Tower, and are now home to the Fusiliers' Museum. The last building commissioned during the nineteenth century was a new Main Guard, a large four-storey structure built in a Jacobean style to the north of the Wakefield Tower between 1898 and 1900.

Although the Tower's displays of arms and armour remained a great draw to the public, by this time the importance of the garrison and arsenal had started to decline, and many of the associated buildings had been destroyed during the 'restoration' of the fortress during the Victorian period. The Second World War wiped out some of those that had survived.

154. (left) The Duke of Wellington laying the foundation stone of the Waterloo Barracks in 1845. Later named after his most famous victory, this vast new building was erected on the site of the Grand Storehouse and could accommodate 1000 men.

155. (top) A detail of a musket lock that was assembled at the Tower c. 1785. It is marked with the word 'Tower' and the cypher of George III.

156. The New Horse Armoury, c. 1870. The staircase on the right led up to the Spanish Armoury, a collection of fearsome-looking weapons and a few instruments of torture, allegedly taken from the Armada of 1588.

The Tower Restored

During the eighteenth century, a growing interest in medieval history had sparked a revival of Gothic architecture, albeit in a rather romanticized form. This revival found full expression in the Victorian era, by which time the meticulous study of medieval buildings inspired much more faithful re-creations. The neo-Gothic age had arrived, and it would have a dramatic impact on the Tower (fig. 160).

Anthony Salvin, a respected architect, was subsequently appointed to carry out a number of other improvements or 'restorations' at the Tower. He was also tasked with making the Beauchamp Tower suitable for the public display of the sixteenth- and seventeenth-century prisoners' inscriptions inside. After studying the building with great care, Salvin had two warders' houses that partially obscured the east front pulled down. Meanwhile, the battlements were re-created, the exterior walls refaced and the windows and doors replaced. The result was to return the tower to its medieval glory (figs. 158 and 159).

As the reign of Queen Victoria (1837–1901) progressed, public interest in the Tower increased considerably. This was at least partly due to the publication in 1840 of *The Tower of London*, a romantic novel by the popular author William Harrison Ainsworth. For many years,

157. (previous pages) A detail of the Tower in 1826 by J. Tugman; see fig. 160.

158. (right) The Beauchamp Tower shortly before Anthony Salvin began his restoration in 1852. By this time, only the pointed hood-moulding over the central window betrayed its thirteenth-century origins.

159. (opposite) The Beauchamp Tower in 1898. The tower was built by Edward I in 1281. All of the later accretions were stripped away by Salvin, and the windows, battlements and other features were restored to what he believed to be their original appearance.

The Tower Restored

160. *The Tower in 1826 by J. Tugman, showing the extent to which the medieval fortress had disappeared under a mass of later buildings.*

the White Tower had been one of the most visited parts of the Tower, but Victoria gradually encouraged access to more of its treasures. The Jewel House was a popular attraction, as were the Armouries and Ordnance stores. In 1838 a ticket office was created out of three old animal cages at the western entrance, where visitors could buy refreshments and an official guidebook (fig. 161). By the end of 1839, the Tower was welcoming 80,000 visitors per year. The introduction of free admission on certain days in 1875 sparked an increase of more than half a million visitors per year. The Tower's emerging role as a visitor attraction was not welcomed by everyone. As Constable, the Duke of Wellington believed that the Tower should be filled with soldiers, not visitors, given its traditional role as a fortress. But he was increasingly outnumbered.

Among the early visitors to the Tower was Victoria's husband, Prince Albert. Keenly interested in architecture, he had come to see the Salt Tower, which was in a state of near-collapse. He concluded that it should be carefully restored to its original condition, but that the work should be carried out as part of a more ambitious

161. *The Tower's first purpose-built ticket office (1851), which included lavatories and a refreshment room. The modern-day ticket office is located on the same site, close to the main (western) entrance to the fortress.*

restoration of the medieval defences. After the success of the Beauchamp Tower restoration, Salvin was again selected for the task, and between 1858 and 1869 he undertook a series of thoroughgoing repairs and improvements that encompassed the Salt Tower, the White Tower and its chapel, St Thomas's Tower, the Bloody Tower and the Wakefield Tower (fig. 163).

Salvin's restoration may have been on a grand scale, but it had also been rooted in scholarly research to ensure that it was both authentic and respectful of the Tower's rich and complex history. The same was not true of the sweeping changes made by his immediate successor, John Taylor, who ruthlessly destroyed a number of important buildings at the Tower because they did not conform to his own ideals of medieval architecture. One of his first projects, begun in 1876, was the restoration of the Chapel of St Peter ad Vincula, which was by then seriously dilapidated. Working to Salvin's original plans, Taylor went far beyond structural repairs, and by the end of his works the

162. One of the last views of the Tower moat filled with water, c. 1840. Three years later, it was decided that its stagnant waters were so polluted with human waste that it constituted a health risk and should be filled in.

eighteenth-century gallery and box pews, and the Baroque pulpit, reading desk and reredos had all been ripped out (figs. 164 and 165). This was typical of church renovations elsewhere during the Victorian era, which resulted in the creation of comparatively lifeless interiors. In the progress of the works at St Peter ad Vincula, the remains of Anne Boleyn and several other executed notables were discovered in the chancel. Their names are now displayed on a plaque inside the chapel.

In 1879 Taylor demolished the large stone building on the east side of the White Tower, which probably dated from the fourteenth century (shown in figs. 66 and 145), along with much of the twelfth-century Wardrobe Tower, which had nestled in its south-east angle. He also oversaw the building of a new Lanthorn Tower to replace the old one, which had been badly damaged by fire in 1774 and demolished two years later. Most contentious of all his schemes, however, was the 'reconstruction' of the inner curtain wall between the Salt and Wakefield towers. This involved the demolition of the Record Office attached to the Wakefield Tower and its replacement with a new curtain wall. What Taylor failed to realize was that the front of this building was part of the thirteenth-century curtain wall, and the rooms behind and above it were important remnants of the medieval palace.

This would be the last phase of the Victorian restoration at the Tower. By the 1890s, the Society for the Protection of Ancient Buildings had successfully argued against any further attempts to 'remedievalize' the Tower, and instead won 'respect for genuine remains of former times'.

163. The Salt Tower in 1846, during the demolition of various buildings put up against it after its creation by Henry III in the thirteenth century.

The Story of The Tower of London

164. *The interior of the Chapel of St Peter ad Vincula before the alterations of 1876–77 stripped away the seventeenth-century reredos and eighteenth-century pews and gallery.*

165. *The chapel interior after the works, which introduced uniform rows of pews and thus increased the capacity of the congregation.*

The Tower Restored

A Living Palace

By the dawn of the twentieth century, the Tower's role as a military fortress and state prison seemed to have been permanently replaced by that as a visitor attraction and ancient monument. But all of that changed with the outbreak of the First World War in 1914.

One of the first prisoners of the war to be housed at the Tower was Carl Hans Lody, a German naval officer who arrived in Britain at the beginning of the war, posing as an American. Part of a network of German spies who were posted to key strategic positions across the country, Lody had been briefed to gather information about a fleet of warships anchored at Rosyth naval base near Edinburgh. His true identity was discovered by MI5, and he was tried by a court martial in London and condemned to death. He spent the night before his

166. (previous pages) The Royal Marines Band on Tower Green during the Ceremony of the Constable's Dues.

167. The North Bastion after being struck by a German bomb on 5 October 1940. The occupant, Yeoman Warder Reeves, lost his life during the incident.

A Living Palace

169. The chair used for the execution of Josef Jakobs, a German spy, in 1941. The Tower housed numerous prisoners of war during both the First and Second World Wars.

execution at the Tower and wrote a touching last letter to his family, telling them: 'Tomorrow I shall be shot here in the Tower. I have had just judges, and I shall die as an officer, not as a spy. Farewell. God bless you.' Lody was the first of eleven spies to be executed by firing squad in the fortress during the war.

The Tower emerged unscathed from the First World War, but it suffered badly from the aerial bombardment of the Second World War. On 23 September 1940, shortly after the 'Blitz' had begun, a number of high-explosive bombs were dropped on the fortress, destroying large sections of the Mint and the Old Hospital Block to the east of the White Tower. More raids followed in October, blowing apart the massive North Bastion and only narrowly missing the White Tower itself (fig. 167).

In May 1941 the Tower received its last high-profile prisoner, when Hitler's right-hand man, Rudolf Hess, was brought to London after landing unexpectedly in Scotland, possibly on a peace mission. He was housed in the Queen's House, and spent a comfortable four days there before being transferred to a series of safe houses. Tried at Nuremberg in 1946, he was sentenced to spend the rest of his days in Berlin's Spandau jail. He died there in 1987.

After the war, once the damage to the Tower had been made good, it reopened as a tourist attraction (fig. 171). From that time onwards,

170. Second World War allotments in the Tower moat. During the war much of the moat was converted into vegetable allotments by the residents of the fortress. After the moat had been drained, it became a training ground for soldiers stationed at the Tower.

171. Visitors return to the Tower of London after the end of the Second World War. The Tower is visibly scarred by the effects of war, and armed soldiers patrol the site. On the left are the remains of the Main Guard, which was destroyed by incendiary devices in 1940.

The Story of The Tower of London

172. (left) A gun salute on Tower wharf, continuing a tradition established at least as early as the 1530s. Salutes are fired on royal anniversaries (such as the Queen's Diamond Jubilee in 2012), on the State Opening of Parliament and to mark visits by foreign heads of state.

173. Beating the Bounds, 1927. Performed every three years on Ascension Day, this event derives from a centuries-old boundary dispute between the Tower and its nearest neighbours. Although lying outside the castle walls, the boundary was considered to be part of the Tower and vital for its security.

this became its principal function and it remains so today. In 1988 the fortress gained World Heritage Site status in recognition of its enormous historical significance.

In 1994 the Royal Logistic Corps withdrew from the Tower, which brought to an end one of its oldest and most important roles as a military supply base. The garrison, meanwhile, has dwindled to a small contingent retained for guard and ceremonial duties. Much of the collection of arms and armour has been transferred to the Royal Armouries in Leeds, although there is still a substantial display of treasured items in the White Tower.

But the Tower remains very much a living fortress, adapting chameleon-like to its changed circumstances while preserving centuries of tradition (figs. 172 and 173). Around 150 people live at the Tower today, most of whom are the famous Yeoman Warders, or 'Beefeaters', and their families, under the command of the Resident Governor of the Tower of London and Keeper of

174. The Stone Kitchen tavern, which once stood on Mint Street, between the Byward and Bell towers. From at least the late seventeenth century until its closure in 1846, it was a popular facility for the Tower's community.

175. A late eighteenth-century pewter tankard once belonging to Yeoman Warder Francis Dobson. The tankard is inscribed with his name and that of the Stone Kitchen tavern. It was dug up in the 1990s near the Bell Tower.

the Jewel House (fig. 168). There is something of a village atmosphere among the residents, all of whom know one another. The spiritual needs of the Tower community are served by the Chapel of St Peter ad Vincula and its resident chaplain. There is also a doctor on site, and a pub for the use of the Yeoman Warders – and a few lucky guests.

Today's Yeoman Warders are required to have served in the armed forces with an honourable record for at least twenty-two years before they can take up residence in the Tower. They must also have reached the rank of warrant officer, have been awarded the Long Service and Good Conduct medal, and be aged between forty and fifty-five years old on appointment. As well as their official duties, such as the Ceremony of the Keys, they also ensure the safety of visitors to the Tower and conduct tours for thousands of tourists every day (fig. 176). For normal duties the Yeoman Warders wear the blue 'undress' uniform, but for ceremonial occasions they don the distinctive red dress uniform, complete with Tudor ruff.

One of the warders holds the position of Ravenmaster. Legend has it that the kingdom and the Tower will fall if the six resident ravens ever leave the fortress (fig. 178). According to tradition, Charles II first decreed that the ravens should be protected. This met with the disapproval of his astronomer, John Flamsteed, who complained that the ravens interfered

176. A Yeoman Warder shows the scaffold site to a group of visitors in 1895. Although the fortress has become synonymous with executions, no permanent scaffold existed, and at most only seven such events took place within the Tower.

with his observatory in the White Tower.

In order to keep the birds at the Tower, their wings are clipped – although that has failed to prevent some escapees in recent years. A raven named Grog turned up outside an East End pub. Today there are seven ravens (one spare), who are very well cared for by the Ravenmaster. Their diet consists of 170 grams (6 oz) of raw meat a day, as well as bird biscuits soaked with blood. They also enjoy an egg once a week, the occasional rabbit (with fur) and scraps of fried bread. But the ravens are expected to earn their comfortable living with good behaviour. When Raven George developed a taste for television aerials, he was dismissed from duty.

The departure of most of the fortress's former institutions has enabled Historic Royal Palaces – the independent charity that looks after

177. (left) In 2012 the Olympic Games took place in London. Many famous landmarks hosted events and celebrations. The Tower of London was the first venue in the capital to host the Olympic flame, which also visited another Historic Royal Palace, Hampton Court.

178. Two of the Tower's resident ravens.

179. Queen Elizabeth II celebrated her Diamond Jubilee in 2012. The Tower played a key role in the commemorations, notably the river pageant from Wandsworth Bridge to Tower Bridge.

180. (below) In 2014, to mark the centenary of the beginning of the First World War, the Tower moat was filled with 888,246 ceramic poppies, each one representing a British military fatality during the conflict. Blood Swept Lands and Seas of Red *was the brainchild of ceramic artist Paul Cummins, and rapidly became one of the most iconic landmarks in London, visited by millions of people from around the globe.*

181. Artist Kendra Haste created life-size sculptures of the royal beasts once kept at the Tower, which were installed throughout the fortress in 2011 and continue to surprise and enthral visitors today. They include a crouching lion, a polar bear tethered by a chain and an elephant peering through an archway.

the Tower of London, Hampton Court Palace, the Banqueting House, Kensington Palace, Kew Palace and Hillsborough Castle – to open up more of the fortress to visitors than ever before. As well as the ever-popular Crown Jewels and White Tower, visitors can enjoy spectacular views of the fortress and riverside from the wall walks, explore the history of the Mint in the buildings where it was once housed, and

The Story of The Tower of London

catch glimpses of the royal beasts in the Brick Tower (fig. 181). People come from all of the world to discover the Tower's myriad stories and tread in the footsteps of some of history's most famous (and notorious) characters: from Anne Boleyn and her daughter, Elizabeth I, to the conspirator Guy Fawkes and the audacious jewel thief Colonel Blood. Some of the most momentous events of our past have been played out inside the walls of the fortress. This is undoubtedly the secret of its enduring appeal.

The Tower of London is now the most popular historic attraction in the United Kingdom, welcoming a staggering 2.5 million visitors each year. It owes its success – and its survival – to its extraordinary ability to adapt to an ever-changing world. Although no longer subject to bombardment from invaders, the fortress is nevertheless subject to the steady encroachment of the City's new high-rise buildings (fig. 182). Yet still it stands, a bastion of the past that is instantly recognizable across the world. We think we must by now know all there is to know about the Tower, but we are always finding out more. A programme of continuous research, conservation and interpretation will ensure that the story of this iconic monument will continue to evolve for centuries to come.

182. Tower Green. The timber-framed Queen's House is in the centre, and on the left are two warders' houses built by Anthony Salvin in the 1860s. The Shard can be seen in the distance.

Further Reading

John Bayley, *The History and Antiquities of the Tower of London*, 2 vols., London, 1829

C.E. Challis (ed.), *A New History of the Royal Mint*, Cambridge (Cambridge University Press) 1992

Daniel Hahn, *The Tower Menagerie: The Amazing True Story of the Royal Collection of Wild and Ferocious Beasts*, London (Simon & Schuster) 2004

Edward Impey (ed.), *The White Tower*, New Haven, Conn., and London (Yale University Press) 2008

— and Geoffrey Parnell, *The Tower of London: The Official Illustrated History*, 2nd rev. edn, London (Merrell/Historic Royal Palaces) 2011

Lucy Inglis, *Georgian London: Into the Streets*, London (Viking) 2013

Fiona Jerome, *Tales from the Tower: Secrets and Stories from a Gory and Glorious Past*, London (Think Books) 2006

Nigel Jones, *Tower: An Epic History of the Tower of London*, London (Hutchinson) 2011

Anna Keay, *The Crown Jewels*, London (Thames & Hudson) 2011

—, *The Elizabethan Tower of London: The Haiward and Gascoyne Plan of 1597*, London (London Topographical Society) 2001

Prisoners of the Tower, Surrey (Historic Royal Palaces) 2009

Index

The Story of The Tower of London

Acknowledgements

I am very grateful for the help and advice of the curatorial team and Tower experts at Historic Royal Palaces, in particular Sally Dixon-Smith, Miranda Garrett, Megan Gooch, Alden Gregory, George Roberts and Jane Spooner. Thanks are also due to Clare Murphy for leading the project on behalf of Historic Royal Palaces, to Sue Mennell for her excellent picture research, and to James Brittain and Nick Guttridge for photography. The team at Merrell has provided unfailing support for the book, in particular Claire Chandler for her meticulous editing, Nicola Bailey for design, and Elizabeth of Mar for publicity. I am also indebted to the work of Dr Edward Impey and Dr Geoffrey Parnell, whose *Tower of London: The Official Illustrated History* was the predecessor of this new study.

Picture Credits

First published 2015 by Merrell Publishers,
London and New York

Merrell Publishers Limited
70 Cowcross Street
London EC1M 6EJ
merrellpublishers.com

in association with

Historic Royal Palaces
Hampton Court Palace
Surrey KT8 9AU
hrp.org.uk

British Library Cataloguing in Publication Data.
A catalogue record for this book is available from
the British Library.

ISBN 978-1-8589-4633-7 (hardback)
ISBN 978-1-8589-4632-0 (paperback)

Produced by Merrell Publishers Limited
Designed by Nicola Bailey
Project-managed by Claire Chandler
Indexed by Hilary Bird

Printed and bound in China

Front jacket/cover:
*The Tower of London seen from the south, across
the River Thames*

Back jacket/cover:
A view of Blood Swept Lands and Seas of Red
by Paul Cummins, 2014

Back endpaper/inside back cover:
Cranmer, at the Traitor's Gate *by Frederick Goodall,
1856 (see fig. 105)*

Frontispiece:
Yeoman Warders on the Middle Drawbridge

Pages 4–5, top to bottom:
*The Tower in a late fifteenth-century book of poems (see
fig. 39); Oratory of St Thomas's Tower (see fig. 51); Traitors'
Gate; The 'Princes in the Tower', after Paul Delaroche, 1831
(see fig. 90); Grand Storehouse fire, 1841 (see fig. 149); Chief
Yeoman Warder in state dress (see fig. 168)*